Fundamentals
of Music

PRENTICE-HALL INTERNATIONAL, INC., *London*

PRENTICE-HALL OF AUSTRALIA, PTY., LTD., *Sydney*

PRENTICE-HALL OF CANADA, LTD., *Toronto*

PRENTICE-HALL OF INDIA (PRIVATE) LTD., *New Delhi*

PRENTICE-HALL OF JAPAN, INC. *Tokyo*

SECOND EDITION

Fundamentals of Music

RAYMOND ELLIOTT

Professor of Music
Texas Technological College

Prentice-Hall, Inc.

Englewood Cliffs, New Jersey

144341

Printed in the United States of America
C-34129

To a quartet of little women
  whose love and devotion made this book possible

  Annie Earl, mother
Helen Gould, wife
  Roberta Annette, daughter
Phyllis Rae, daughter

Preface

The second edition of *Fundamentals of Music* contains many suggestions from teachers some of whom have used the book since its publication a decade ago. Although there are many improvements in the text and musical examples, the most apparent changes are as follows:

1. *Chord progressions* for a foundation in keyboard experience and harmonic ear training. This material is treated in four ways:

(a) conventional progressions of the principal and secondary chords in the major and minor modes;

(b) application of the chord material in the harmonization of a melody with the chord tones in both bass and treble;

(c) the melody in the treble with chord tones in the bass;

(d) the harmonization of an additional melody in which close and open chord structures are stressed. The latter is for observation and study. Passing and neighboring tones are identified in all of the melodies harmonized.

2. *Chordal accompaniment* which is closely related to the above is another important addition. Many chording rhythmic patterns are introduced and the student is shown how to apply these to the melodies found in each chapter.

This book is designed to integrate theory, music-reading, and melodic ear-training. Its aim is to lay the foundations of musicianship through emphasis upon hearing and seeing rhythm and melody with a suggestion of their harmonic background. For the simplest and most effective presentation, a fundamental pattern is followed in each chapter.

The first part of each chapter deals with the rudiments of music. The elementary theoretical aspects of music are introduced and applied as needed. Thus scales, keys, time signatures, melodic design, and chords are woven through each chapter, making them an integral part of the music itself.

Harmony is the next consideration in each chapter. Since most melodic skips are made between the members of a chord, each new tonal problem is approached through the triad. The chord, with its passing and neighboring tones, is first presented and then immediately applied in the Melodies for Singing and Dictation. One of the chief factors in the selection of the melodies for each chapter was consideration of the particular chords and the intervals between their components. This, of course, does not mean that no other chords are implied in the melody; it simply means that the important emphasis is placed on the intervals of the chords under consideration. The new chord introduced in each chapter, with those presented previously, is indicated with Roman numerals in a few of the melodies. These should be played as the melodies are sung. The purpose of this procedure is to impart an introductory feeling for the harmonic background of melody. For further aid in hearing melodic intervals and harmony, the chords should be sung in arpeggio form.

The next division in each chapter is concerned with rhythm. Although most people have a natural response to meter in general, they are frequently weak in perceiving and responding to rhythmic patterns as represented by notation in the music score. One way to strengthen the response to rhythmic patterns is the use of isolated rhythm drills which are to be tapped and counted. The author believes that such isolation is unnecessary and that rhythms should invariably be presented in a tonal setting. But in order that a minimum of difficulty is experienced, only one new rhythmic problem is introduced in each chapter. Rhythm as well as harmony has thus been incorporated as an important consideration in the selection of melodies for each chapter.

As has already been implied, the Melodies for Singing and Dictation, the next chapter division, contain the tonal and rhythmic problems introduced in each chapter.

The final chapter division contains suggestions for further study followed by a work sheet.

A NOTE ON MUSIC-READING

Music is a language, and for its fullest appreciation and comprehension one must achieve mastery of its techniques. The ability to read and understand music depends upon both the ear and the eye. The hearing must precede the eye for it is impossible to sing tones we cannot hear. In this respect it is like learning our mother tongue: we learn to speak it, by imitating what is heard, before learning to read it. It is only later that we learn the signs and symbols which represent sounds and objects. This is precisely the procedure in learning to hear and see music. And, as in language, it implies more than a recognition of symbols, for comprehension is the important essential; and comprehension involves a study of the structure of either language or music. The first approach to reading music, then, is through listening, for music is an aural art. The second is through the eye; as in reading we comprehend through recognition of printed symbols, so in music we comprehend meaning through recognition of individual music notations.

The first attempts at reading music can hardly be called sight-singing. Many repetitions are necessary for both ear and eye for easy recognition of tonal and rhythmic patterns with their various positions on the staff. The beginner consequently must master these patterns for fluency. The developing process of these fundamental skills is not sight-singing as such, but simply ear and eye training. Skill in music-reading develops gradually as the student reads more and more widely in various styles of music.

Although a general resemblance between reading a language and reading music has been pointed out, the specific problems in reading music are actually different from those in book reading since the habits and skills necessary to meet the requirements of good reading are different. Let us consider briefly three of the major differences.

1. In reading music the student must develop a feeling for the key. This means that he must hear the tonal relationship existing between the several tones of the key. He must hear, first, individual tones, then must aurally comprehend several at a time, as a group: a succession of tones as in melody, a group simultaneously as in harmony. The ear must learn to respond to about as many melodic intervals as there are letters in the English alphabet. The main difference between the phonetic qualities of alphabetical sounds and melodic intervals is that musical sounds exist in pitch relationship at a definite pitch and alphabetical sounds do not. This particular complexity calls for special training not at all required in book reading.

2. The act of seeing in music-reading is also more involved than in language. In music, the span of vision is one of breadth as well as linear dimension. In book reading the vertical distance is restricted to the height of the letters. Furthermore, the eye moves along in a single horizontal line, though this is by groups or "eye spans" rather than a single progression. In contrast, in reading music, the eye moves not only horizontally but vertically as well, and at many angles. Thus the problem is more complex spatially, the area varying between one-fourth and one-third of an inch; in other words, the distance from the space below the staff to the space above the staff.[1] Reading piano or orchestral scores is even more involved.

[1] Otto Ortman, "Span of Vision in Note Reading," *Music Educators National Conference*, 1937, p. 88.

3. Music offers a fundamental difference in the matter of rhythm. For example, the student must retain tones for definite lengths of time, at the same time anticipating, with appropriate comprehension, the pitch and length of tones following. There are about as many different note lengths as there are letters in the alphabet, and their combinations further complicate matters. Add these problems to those presented by intervals, and it will be easy to understand why the student must be mentally alert in order to hear and see music.

ACKNOWLEDGMENTS

Acknowledgment is due the following publishers for use of melodies as follows:

Silver Burdett Company, Volume I of *The Progressive Music Series:* "Little Sister's Lullaby," p. 206; "Happy Thoughts," p. 219; "Polly's Bonnet," p. 189; "The Postman," p. 190; "Honey Bee," p. 245; "The Skipping Rope," p. 204; "At the Dance," p. 126; "Street Music," p. 226; "In May Time," p. 291; "In Wooden Shoes," p. 214; "Thanksgiving Day," p. 284; Valentine Song," p. 216; "The Little Seeds," p. 133; "The Mulberry Bush," p. 199; "The Flower's Friend," p. 223; "Night and Morning," p. 297; "The Wizard," p. 299; "The Oriole's Nest," p. 236; "A Cat-Land Law," p. 288. Volume II of *The Progressive Music Series:* "New Day," p. 141; "Solitude," p. 190; "The Homesick Lowlander," p. 162; "The Raindrops," p. 233; "Noel," p. 263; "The Rainbow Dress," p. 182; "The Old Shepherd," p. 200; "In the Sleigh," p. 197; "Guessing Song," p. 140; "Dance of the Leaves," p. 188. From Volume III of *The Progressive Music Series:* "The Old Apple Tree," p. 184; "Happy Autumn Days," p. 143; "Summer's Done," p. 140; "In Ocean Cave," p. 198; "The Frost," p. 139; "My Bonny Pipes," p. 142; "Well Met, Well Met," p. 152; "The Maypole," p. 138; "Come, Lassies and Lads," p. 159.

C. C. Birchard Company, *Senior Laurel Songs:* "Peace Be With All," p. 125, Lithuanian Melody, arrangement by Hunt; "Pastoral," p. 157, Peruvian Folk Tune, arrangement by Winthrop; "The Three Sons," p. 13, Somerset Folk Song, arrangement by Hunt; "Carem Carmela," p. 228, Mexican Folk Tune, arrangement by Spaulding. *The School Song Book:* "A Life on the Ocean Wave," p. 33, by Russell.

American Book Company, *Hollis Dann Song Series,* Book Two: "In Spring," by Busch, p. 88, and for checking the copyright status of many melodies found in their publications.

Permission for reprint of "Obstination" by H. de Fontenailles granted by Duran et Cie, Paris, France; Elkan-Vogel Co., Inc., Philadelphia 3, Pennsylvania, Agents.

Heugel et Cie for reprint of "Elegy" by Massenet.

For their help in preparing this book grateful acknowledgment is made to the following: Professor Howard A. Murphy, Teachers College, Columbia University; Dr. Walter E. Nallin, City College of New York; Dr. Everett A. Gillis, Helen Elliott, Mary Jeanne van Appledorn, Dr. Gene Hemmle, Texas Technological College; Earl L. Weidner, New Jersey State Teachers College; Dr. Rogers Whitmore, University of Missouri; Raymond Stuhl, Jeannette Cass Stough, University of Kansas; Mildred Cook McClintock and Dow Mooney.

RAYMOND ELLIOTT

Analytic Table of Contents

Analytic Table of Contents (continued)

Analytic Table of Contents (continued)

Contents

1

Tone and Its Representation

Music is a medium of expressing thought and feeling through tone and time. It is an art, and all forms of art are means through which beauty is expressed. The medium employed for the expression determines the type of art. Where the painter uses lines and color as his medium, and the sculptor uses stone or metal, the musician uses *tone* and *time*. Through these media he transfers his thoughts, emotions, and moods to others. He organizes his feelings and expresses them through the three elements of music—*rhythm, melody,* and *harmony*—whose combination is called *form.*

Tone. *Tone* is the result of regular vibrations. Irregular vibrations produce noise. A musical tone has four characteristics: namely, *pitch, length, quality,* and *quantity.* The *pitch* is determined by the number of vibrations per second: the higher the tone, the greater the number of vibrations per second; the lower the tone, the fewer the number of vibrations. The *length* or *duration* of the tone has to do with the interval of time during which the vibrations continue. The *quality* or *timbre* is concerned with the character or kind of tone produced. That is, tonal quality is determined by the producing instrument and its resonating capacity. The *quantity* or *intensity* refers to the degree of strength, force, or volume of the tone.

It is quite evident that the musician has a wide range in his media of tone and time. If he writes for a single voice, his choice of tone is naturally limited to the range and quality of that particular voice. This is also true of a single instrument, with the exception of one with a very wide range, such as the piano. But when he is writing for a group of voices or instruments he is practically unlimited. Considering the timbre and range of the various voices and instruments, and the many combinations of their qualities and tones at different pitches and lengths, it is almost impossible to imagine the complexity of the material which the composer has at his disposal.

The task confronting us, then, is to train the ear, the eye, and the mind to comprehend this tonal material. To do this—that is, to acquire the ability to respond accurately to the four characteristics of tone—requires time, patience, concentration, self-analysis, and constructive criticism. Only those who put forth the necessary effort to obtain this skill earn the right to the title of musician, for such expertness is the essence of *musicianship*. From the very beginning, the student must approach the art with a scientific attitude, and his advance should be marked by accuracy and precision.

Notation.   *Notation* is the representation of music on paper. The system with which we are so familiar, as is true of any language, was hundreds of years in the making. At first, music was transmitted orally, to the ear only; but as the art grew more complex, a means of conveying it to the eye was necessary. The result was the development of a system of signs by which the composer could convey his musical ideas to others.

As an approach to understanding this system of signs, let us begin with the piano keyboard. The black keys, it will be observed, are in alternate groups of twos and threes, the other keys being white. Begin on the white key to the left of two black keys and play the closing phrase of the well-known hymn *God of Our Fathers,* using white keys only. Let your ear direct your fingers in this descending passage. Now sing the phrase.

Ex. 1-1

WARREN

The tones you played and sang are represented on the *staff* as shown in Ex. 1-1. The staff is a group of five parallel lines on which *notes* and *rests* are placed. Each line and each space is called a *degree,* of which there are *degree.*

nine—five lines and four spaces. The staff may be extended when needed by adding short lines called *ledger lines* above and below the regular lines. The degrees are numbered as follows:

Ex. 1-2

	2nd space above	2nd ledger line above
5th line	1st space above	1st ledger line above
4th line	4th space	
3rd line	3rd space	
2nd line	2nd space	
1st line	1st space	
	1st space below	1st ledger line below
	2nd space below	2nd ledger line below

It will be observed from Ex. 1-1 that the letters above the notes follow an alphabetical order. This is due to the fact that the first seven letters of the alphabet are used to name the lines and spaces, as well as the keys of the piano (see Ex. 1-6). Since the staff would have little meaning if each degree did not represent a definite pitch, a sign called a *clef* is used. The one used in Ex. 1-1 is known as the G clef, its name and form being derived from the Gothic letter G, a resemblance to which can be seen in our capital letter by the same name. When the G clef is placed on the second line of the staff (so said because it crosses it four times), it indicates that the second line of the staff is G, the first G *above* middle C. The latter is the white key to the left of two black keys nearest the center of the piano keyboard. The letter names of the other staff degrees are calculated from G, following an alphabetical order as shown below:

Ex. 1-3

Also in common use is the F clef[1] which originates on the fourth line of the staff, indicating that this line is F, the first F *below* middle C. It, too, originates from the Gothic, resembling our capital letter F. The letter

[1] The *C* clef **ⅠƁ Ⱨ Ⅰƃ** locates Middle *C* on any line of the staff. When placed on the third line, it is known as the alto clef; and when placed on the fourth line, the tenor clef. It is often used with orchestral instruments.

names of the other staff degrees are calculated from F, again following an alphabetical order as shown below:

Ex. 1-4

The staffs using both the G and F clefs are often connected by a *brace* shown below which indicates that the music so joined is to be performed simultaneously, thus:

Ex. 1-5

The staff employing the G clef is often called the *treble* staff, meaning high. Although not always, the right hand usually performs the music written on this staff for the piano.

Similarly, the staff using the F clef is sometimes called the *bass* staff, meaning low. As a general rule the left hand plays the notation for the piano on this staff.

The combination of the bass and treble staffs, as shown in Ex. 1-6, is known as the *great staff*. The duplication beginning on each eighth key of the piano and the eighth letter of the staff is important. It is a repetition which occurs regularly throughout the entire piano keyboard and on the staff. The difference in pitch between any letter name on the staff, or any key name on the piano, to the next corresponding letter or key, either up or down, is called an *octave* (eight), for example: C, C; D, D; E, E; and so on. Observe also the names of the various octave groups, beginning on C. Any pitch within a given octave is named from the C immediately below it, thus: first space below bass staff is great F; fourth line, bass, small F; first space, treble, F^1 and so forth.

It will be observed from Ex. 1-6 that only the white keys have corresponding lines and spaces. The black keys, as will be seen later, derive their names from the white keys and are represented on the staff by sharps and flats.

Ex. 1-6

Returning to Ex. 1-1, let us center our attention on the tones of this phrase which are contained in the C-octave. This succession of tones is known as a *scale,* which may be in an ascending or a descending order as shown at (a) and (b) in Ex. 1-7. Much of our music is founded upon this series of tones. Still other tones, which we shall study later, are derived from this series.

Ex. 1-7

These tones are related to each other by natural laws of sound and their relationships must become so thoroughly familiar that we can hear any tone of the series from any other given tone. This, the first important step in ear training, can be accomplished only by training ourselves to hear the allied tones. It means that we must practice identifying each tone by its distinct character and by its relationship to each of the others. It must be remembered that the ability to read music depends on the accuracy with which the ear can identify sounds, for it is impossible to sing tones we cannot hear. The ear, then, is the singer's guide. We learn to sing by imitating what we hear, much as we learn to speak a language; since the series of tones given above is the foundation of the musical language, we must learn to imitate and recognize their sounds perfectly.

Singing Ex. 1-1 again, it will be observed that the tones are of various duration, the last being the longest. As a whole, the note-lengths seem to be related by time. This may be experienced by regularly repeating the counts *one, two, three, four* as the melody is played. We may conclude that time in music is reckoned by a system of notes representing *relative* time values, and by assigning a *count* to a given note. This will be more fully developed in the next chapter. At the moment, we are concerned with the system of note-lengths as employed in modern notation, shown below:

Ex. 1-8

Eighth - - - - - - - 𝅘𝅥𝅮 𝅘𝅥𝅮 𝅘𝅥𝅮 𝅘𝅥𝅮 𝅘𝅥𝅮 𝅘𝅥𝅮 𝅘𝅥𝅮 𝅘𝅥𝅮

Sixteenth - - - - - - 𝅘𝅥𝅯 𝅘𝅥𝅯 𝅘𝅥𝅯 𝅘𝅥𝅯 𝅘𝅥𝅯 𝅘𝅥𝅯 𝅘𝅥𝅯 𝅘𝅥𝅯 𝅘𝅥𝅯 𝅘𝅥𝅯 𝅘𝅥𝅯 𝅘𝅥𝅯 𝅘𝅥𝅯 𝅘𝅥𝅯 𝅘𝅥𝅯 𝅘𝅥𝅯

Thirty-second - - - - - 𝅘𝅥𝅰

These symbols, representing tone lengths, are sometimes called *relative note-lengths* because each succeeding note is a fractional part of the whole note, and the time value is reckoned accordingly. For example, if four equal counts are given to the whole note, then the half note will receive two counts of the same length, the quarter one count, the eighth one-half of a count, and so on.

The round part of the note is called the *head,* the line attached to the head, the *stem,* and the curved line attached to the stem, the *hook.* Eighth, sixteenth, or thirty-second notes are often represented in groups by a straight line or lines attached to the stems, thus: ♩♩ ♫.These lines are called *beams* or *ligatures.*

An increase in the time value of notes may be designated by *dots,* which are placed at the right of the note head and which increase the time value of the note by one-half. That is, the dot receives one-half as much time as the note: ♩· = ♩ + ♩   ♩· = ♩ + 𝅘𝅥𝅮.   Sometimes two dots are used by a note. In this case the second dot is one-half the value of the first, thus:

$$♩·· = ♩ + ♩ + 𝅘𝅥𝅮   ♩·· = ♩ + 𝅘𝅥𝅮 + 𝅘𝅥𝅯$$

The symbols which represent a silent passage of time in music are called *rests;* they correspond to the note time-values. Rests, like notes, may be dotted, the time value increasing in conformity with the rule mentioned above. The following rests are used in modern notation:

Ex. 1–9

Whole - - - - - - - - - - - - - - - - - - - ▬ 2

Half - - - - - - - - - - - ▬   ▬

Quarter - - - - - - - 𝄽   𝄽   𝄽   𝄽

2 The whole rest may be employed in a measure of any meter. See p. 170.

| Eighth | - - - - - - | γ | γ | γ | γ | γ | γ | γ | γ |

Sixteenth - - - - - $\gamma\gamma\gamma\gamma\gamma\gamma\gamma\gamma\gamma\gamma\gamma\gamma\gamma\gamma\gamma\gamma$

Thirty-second - - - γ

Suggestions for Further Study

Play and sing the scale many times in both *treble* and *bass,* using the following letters, syllables, and numerals.

c	d	e	f	g	a	b	c[3]
do	re	me	fa	so	la	ti	do
1	2	3	4	5	6	7	8

Pay particular attention to the relation of each tone to the other. *Listen carefully* to the quality and pitch of the tone produced by the piano and by your own voice, being sure to maintain a critical attitude. If you play any instrument other than the piano, play the scale on it for yourself and for the class, observing the quality of tone.

Play small divisions of the scale, such as *c, d, e; c, e; e, f, g; e, g;* etc. Sing each group immediately after playing. Now reverse the process: first sing small divisions of the scale, then test yourself at the piano. Be as critical of your work as possible. Practice the exercises given above until you can hear the tones of the scale without singing them aloud.

Make a great staff by placing a dotted line representing Middle *C* between the treble and bass staffs. Name the lines and spaces on each staff, indicating their octave group.

Play *c* on the piano; think the pitch of *c*[1]; sing it; play it.

Play *c*[1]; think the pitch of *c;* sing it; play it.

Sound *c*[1] on the piano, and without further aid from the instrument sing other tones of the scale above or below. After each try, test with the piano. Practice this until you can sing any tone of the scale from *c.*

[3] The letters are called *absolute pitch names* because each represents a definite pitch. The syllables and numerals are *relative pitch names,* because any pitch may be used for *do* (1), and because the other tones of the scale take their pitch in relation to the given pitch. The use of syllables is very old, having been employed by the Chinese, Hindus, and ancient Greeks. Our syllables are derived from the system invented by Guido of Arezzo (980-1050), who used the first syllable in each line of a Latin hymn to Saint John the Baptist—*ut, re, mi, fa, sol, la.*

2

Meter and Measure

Meter. Sing the following well-known melody, observing the strong-weak pulsation:

Ex. 2-1

Now sing the following familiar hymn, noting the strong-weak-weak pulsation:

Ex. 2-2

These examples illustrate the basic accents which help to give vitality to music. The first moved in groups of twos (strong-weak), whereas the second was in groups of threes (strong-weak-weak). Such groups, with their schemes of accents, constitute *meter.* In the first example we felt a strong-weak pulsation known as *duple meter;* in the second a strong-weak-weak variety known as *triple meter.*

Measure.   Each pulsation, whether strong or weak, is called a *beat.* The beats, with their regularly recurring accents, are always found in groups of twos or threes, or a combination thereof, and are grouped into uniform *measures.* The *bar,* a perpendicular line drawn across the staff, indicates these groupings. The first beat following it is usually the strong part of the measure, but only in certain styles or periods. Sing the examples above again, observing that the strong accent occurs on the beat immediately following the measure bar.

Returning again to Ex. 2-1, we observe that there are two quarter notes or their equivalent in each measure, in conformance with the numerals $\frac{2}{4}$ found at the beginning of the example. The sign $\frac{2}{4}$ is known as the *metric* or *time signature,* the upper designating the number of beats to be found in each measure and the lower the kind of note which will receive a beat. Reading from the top downward, the signature denotes that there are two beats in each measure and that a beat is to be given to each quarter note. This, then, is in two-four time, or *duple* meter.

In Ex. 2-2 there are three quarter notes or their equivalent between each bar, as indicated by the metric signature. This example, then, is in three-four time, or *triple* meter.

To summarize, it must be remembered that the upper figure in any metric signature indicates the number of beats, pulses, or counts in a measure, and the lower, the kind of note receiving a beat. With this in mind, study the following:

(a) As the melody is played, count two beats (one, two) in each measure, observing that the half note is receiving one beat, as indicated by the time signature.

Ex. 2-3 (a)

Scotland's Burning   Scotch Round

(b) Count four beats in each measure (one, two, three, four), observing that one count or beat is being given to each quarter note which is indicated by the time signature.

Ex. 2-3 (b)

All Through The Night   Welsh Air

(c) Count six beats in each measure, observing that the eighth note is the beat note.

Ex. 2-3 (c)

Drink to Me Only With Thine Eyes   English Air

The lower figure often varies according to the desire of the composer. Take the following for an example:

Ex. 2-4

Two beats in each measure, the half-note receiving a beat.

Two beats in each measure, the quarter-note receiving a beat.

Two beats in each measure, the eighth note receiving a beat.

The selection of a unit or beat-note is purely a matter of choice and in no way affects the speed or character of the music. The illustrations in Ex. 2-4 are merely three different ways of indicating that there are to be two beats in each measure. We might print the word "cat" in a number of different types of letters, but the meaning of the word would remain unchanged. We may conclude, then, that a composition would sound the same whether it were written in $\frac{2}{2}$, $\frac{2}{4}$, or $\frac{2}{8}$.

To get a more vivid picture of these regularly recurring accents, let us compare them with the accents in poetry.

Ex. 2-5

The first-pulse in each group is accented and it occurs at regular time intervals, thereby producing measure.

The six meters in common use are illustrated below.

Ex. 2-6

(a) Duple Meter (Simple—one duple group in each measure)

(b) Triple Meter (Simple—one triple group in each measure)

(c) Quadruple Meter (Simple—one quadruple group in each measure)

(d) Compound Duple Meter—Sextuple
(Two triple groups in each measure)

(e) Compound Triple Meter[1]   (f) Compound Quadruple Meter
(Three triple groups in   (Four triple groups in
each measure)   each measure)

It is necessary for the musician to feel these groups of pulses because they are the foundation for more complex musical patterns. It should be noted, however, that all music does not begin on the accented part of the measure, as the following shows:

Ex. 2-7

Old Hundredth   Bourgeois

Praise God from Whom all   bless - ings flow

[1] Other time signatures such as $\frac{6}{16}$ $\frac{9}{16}$ $\frac{5}{4}$ $\frac{7}{4}$ are possible.

12

Conductor's pattern. An excellent means of learning to feel such groups is to experience the physical manifestation of the conductor's beat. The two most important motions of his hand are (1) the *preliminary* or *preparatory beat* and (2) the *down beat.* The preliminary beat is a "get ready" movement of the hand which precedes the initial beat in the composition. It may be illustrated by the dotted line in the following representation of the conductor's beat pattern for duple and triple meter.

Ex. 2-8

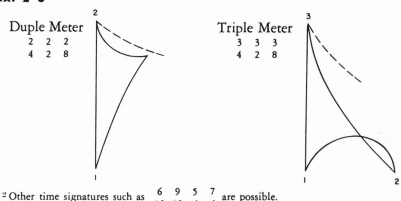

Duple Meter
2 2 2
4 2 8

Triple Meter
3 3 3
4 2 8

² Other time signatures such as $\frac{6}{16} \quad \frac{9}{16} \quad \frac{5}{4} \quad \frac{7}{4}$ are possible.

As may be seen, its direction is determined by the first beat in the composition. If the music begins on count one, the preparatory beat for duple meter originates as if on count two in the conductor's pattern and moves upward into position for the down beat, and for triple meter on count three. If the music begins on the fourth count in quadruple meter as in Ex. 2-7 above, the preparatory beat originates as if on count three and moves to the position for the count of four which begins the piece.² Whether the preliminary beat is quick or slow is determined by the nature of the piece it initiates. If the composition is a march, the "get ready" beat should be quick; if the music is somber, the preparatory beat should so indicate. The purpose of the preliminary beat is to prepare the performers. For singers and wind instrumentalists, it is the signal to breathe; for the violinists and other stringed instrumentalists, to get bow and fingers into position.

Many beginners encounter some difficulty in feeling the preliminary beat. Some have found it helpful to count aloud the beat on which the preliminary beat originates. Others use the words *sing* or *play* to initiate the preparatory beat.

The down beat is definite, confident, expectant. It should move straight down, hit an imaginary base, and bounce in the direction of the following beat. It is with the down beat that the conductor indicates the measure bar, and thus the strongest beat within the measure. It should be different

² The upbeat, the last beat in a measure as in Ex. 2-7, is called *anacrusis.*

and definite enough from other beats to ensure no doubt concerning it. The hand motions and counts for the duple and triple meters have already been given in Ex. 2-8, with the preliminary beat indicated by a dotted line. Use them as you sing Exs. 2-1 and 2-2 at the beginning of this chapter, and continue their use on the Melodies for Singing found later in this chapter.

Meter, rhythm, and tempo.   Because of the confusion existing with reference to the terms meter, rhythm, and tempo, it might be of value at this point to define each briefly, more details being furnished in later chapters. *Meter* may be defined as the scheme of accents. *Rhythm* pertains to everything of a temporal or durational quality of tone, and therefore, in its broadest sense, to the tones and rests of different lengths within the meter. *Tempo* refers to the speed at which a composition is executed. In this regard, it must be emphasized that the metric signature in no way indicates the speed of the beats. The composer uses two primary methods for indicating tempo, but since these will be discussed later, for the present the following terms expressive of tempo will serve our need:

Grave—slow and solemn	Andante—going, moving at
Lento—slow	moderate rate
Largo—large, broad, slow	Allegro—cheerful, quick
Adagio—at ease, leisurely	Vivace—very lively
Moderato—at moderate speed	Presto—very, very lively

Melodies for Singing and Dictation

The following melodies are in duple and triple meter and contain various note and rest lengths. Use the conductor's beat while the melodies are being played, and accent the down beat. Then sing them, using letters, syllables, and numbers. Keep a steady, even beat.

Melodies for Singing

3 Adagio

4 Adagio

5 Allegro

6 Vivace

7 Moderato

8 Andante

9 Andante

15

Melodies for Dictation

Suggestions for Further Study

Sound c^1 on the piano, and without further aid from the instrument, sing other tones of the scale above or below. Test with the piano.

Transcribe on the work sheet below several of the above Melodies for Dictation, substituting the *F* clef for the *G*, and the *G* clef for the *F*.

Write and play the *c* scale, ascending and descending, beginning on the following pitches: C, c, c^1.

Transcribe several of the above Melodies for Dictation, substituting $\frac{2}{4}$ for $\frac{2}{2}$, $\frac{2}{2}$ for $\frac{2}{4}$, $\frac{3}{4}$ for $\frac{3}{2}$, and $\frac{3}{2}$ for $\frac{3}{4}$

Work Sheet

[3] Since melodies 12 and 14 contain only one note in each measure, the teacher should use an accompaniment to aid the student in determining the meter.

3

Major Scales and Keys

Rudiments

Once again, play the last phrase of *God of Our Fathers,* making two important observations:

1. There is no key between C and B, and F and E.
2. There is a key between all other successive keys played.

Ex. 3-1

WARREN

C	B	A	G	G	F	E	D	D	C
8	7	6	5	5	4	3	2	2	1
do	ti	la	so	so	fa	mi	re	re	do [1]

Scale formula. The observations above lead us to a discovery of the scale formula or interval pattern of the scale. An *interval* is the difference in pitch between any two tones. There are, of course, several of these in our musical language, which will be studied later, but for the present we are concerned with only two, the *half step* and the *whole step.*[2] Since piano keys are arranged in half step order, it follows that from any key on the piano to the next key above or below, white or black, is a half step. When there is a key between two keys, the interval is a whole step. Since there was no key between C and B, and F and E in the phrase above, the interval is a half step. The other intervals where there was a key between are whole steps. Thus the formula or interval pattern of the scale is as

---

[1] Since they are widely employed in the public schools, this text uses, in addition to the letter names, both number and Latin syllable names.

[2] Also called semitone and whole tone.

shown below. Since this is the formula for all major scales, it should be committed to memory.

Ex. 3-2

The full name of the scale constructed according to the interval pattern given above is the *major diatonic scale*. It is what we mean when we commonly speak of a scale. The word *scale* comes from the Latin, *scala*, meaning a ladder. The word *major* refers to certain intervals that are larger than the corresponding intervals in the minor scale which will be studied later. *Diatonic* is from the Greek: *dia*, through; and *tonus*, a tone or sound. The word literally means, through the tones of a scale or of a key. Actually the tones belonging to any scale or key are diatonic tones; in this respect the major scale is typical.

We have already learned that the tones of a scale are related to each other and to the key tone. Consequently, we may think of the tones of a scale as representing a *family* of *related* tones called a key.[3] In the scale, ascending or descending, the tones occur in consecutive or alphabetical order, but when arranged in any order, as in melody, and related to a central tone (the key tone), they are said to be tones of a key. Sing Ex. 2-1 and Ex. 2-2 (Chapter 2) again, noting that the tones are drawn to a central tone which seems to be the center of gravity of the key.

Tetrachords. Every scale is divisable into two equal parts called *tetrachords* (Greek: *tetra*, four; and *chord*, a string or note), each of which contains the same intervals, namely, a half step between three and four of each group, and a whole step between the other tones. The two tetrachords are separated by the interval of a step, thus:

Ex. 3-3

[3] The term key as used here is not synonymous with the keys on the piano.

Building new scales.   Thus far we have played, sung, and written the scale from only one degree of the staff, namely C; but a scale may begin on any pitch—any degree of the staff or key on the piano. This pitch, the tone on which it commences, furnishes the name of the scale and is called the *key tone.* For example, the C scale is so named because it begins on C; C is its key tone. When we build a scale on any tone other than C, we follow a similar pattern.

As an approach toward building a scale on a tone other than C, let us sing the familiar phrase from *God of Our Fathers,* beginning on G^2. Does it not sound the same as from C except that the tones are higher? Now play the phrase beginning on G^2, using white keys only. Obviously something was wrong between 8 and 7 of the passage, the error being due to the whole step between 7 and 8. According to the scale formula, this interval should be a half step. The one necessary correction at the piano is the use of a black key for the seventh tone, in order to make the passage sound as it should. In other words, the use of this black key makes the steps and half steps occur at the proper places as may be seen by comparing the intervals with those when beginning on C. It also should be observed that this new series contains all the tones from the series beginning on C except the new black key, and that G A B C formed the upper tetrachord of the scale of C (see Ex. 3-3).

In order to represent the new black key on the staff, it is necessary to place a character called a *sharp* (♯) before the note on *F.* When this symbol is placed on a degree of the staff, it causes that degree to represent a pitch one half step higher. Here is how the new scale appears on the staff and keyboard.

Ex. 3-4

Since *F* sharp is a necessity of the new scale, it becomes an integral part of the key, and is therefore a *diatonic* tone, the new series of tones giving rise to a *new* scale and a *new* key (*G*). When music is written in this key, the sharp is placed on the fifth line of the treble staff and the fourth line of the bass staff, to the right of the clef. This is the sign of the key of *G,*

and is known as the *key signature*. It indicates that each *F* on the staff is to be raised one half step to *F* sharp. Here is how the new scale appears in both the treble and bass staffs:

Ex. 3-5

It should be noted again that, with the single exception of *F* sharp, the scale of *G* has the same tones as the scale of *C*, which suggests that the key of *G* is very closely related to the key of *C*.[5]

Now let us take the upper tetrachord of the scale of *G* for the lower tetrachord of another new scale, the scale of *D*. Sing the scale from *D*. Play it and notice that it is necessary to place a sharp on the seventh tone, *C*, of the new scale. The *F*, it should be noted, is also raised by a sharp, having been carried over in the tetrachord. In fact, all of the tones used were found in the *G* scale except *C* sharp. This suggests again that a close relationship exists between the two scales. The new scale as it appears on the staff and keyboard is shown below:

Ex. 3-6

The *F* sharp and the *C* sharp, being essential to the new key, are integral parts of it; in other words, diatonic tones. Therefore, they are placed

---

[4] Since *G* has become the key tone, the position of do, mi, so, and do (1, 3, 5, and 8) should be observed very carefully.

[5] This relationship is explained more fully on p. 125.

on the staff following the clef in the order of occurrence and form the key signature of the key of *D* major (see p. 21).

Ex. 3-7

The student should familiarize himself with these and other major sharp key signatures. These are shown on page 60. He should note the order of the sharps in the key signature carefully. The following rule may serve as a guide to the identification of the major keys using sharps: the last sharp in the key signature is *ti* (7); the next degree above is *do* (1). The name of the major key is always the same as the degree on which *do* (1) is found.

Characteristics of scale tones. If we study the tonal characteristics and individualities of the tones of the major scale, we find that some of them seem to be unsettled and to have a tendency to lead one to a more restful tone. We are not content to stop on re (2), fa (4), la (6), or ti (7), for any length of time. Re wants to lead us on to do or mi; fa to mi; la to so; and ti to do. These four tones (re, fa, la, ti) are called *active tones,* and they resolve to the *rest tones* do, mi, and so. This does not mean that ti must always resolve to do, fa to mi, or la to so, for they do not always do so. It does mean, however, that unless they move along the scale in the opposite direction in such passages as mi, fa, so; so, la, ti, do; or do, ti, la, so, the chances are they will resolve to their respective rest tones.

Ex. 3-8

Resolution of Active Tones

Harmony

The tonic chord. And now, for the discovery of further aspects of tones of the scale, sing the first part of "The Marine's Hymn."

Ex. 3-9

Allegro   The Marine's Hymn

From the halls of Mon - te - zu - - -

Official Song of the United States Marine Corps

ma, To the shores of Trip- o - - li; _____

When sounded together, the first three tones of this well-known melody form the *tonic* chord, the term *tonic* being used in harmony to designate the *first* tone of the scale. Chords are built by thirds from a tone called the root (see (a) Ex. 3-10). C, the first tone of the scale, is the root of the tonic chord in the key of C. A third above C is E (C D E) and is therefore

                                                 1 2 3

called the third of the chord. The third above E is G. Being a fifth above the root (C D E F G), G is the fifth of the chord. Other thirds may be

           1 2 3 4 5

added to form other types of chords, but for the present we are concerned with a three-tone chord, or *triad*. The particular chord under consideration is referred to as the *tonic* (or I) *triad* as it is a three-tone chord built on the first degree of the scale; it is also known as the C chord or triad. Note that its members are on adjacent lines, or alternate degrees of the staff which is due to the root being on a line. Other chords, which will be studied later, are constructed in like manner. In each case, chord members are on adjacent lines or in spaces, depending on whether the root is located on a line or space.

Although a chord is identified by the arrangement on alternate staff degrees of root, third, and fifth, the chord tones may be arranged in any order.

Ex. 3-10

(a)	(b)	(c)
fifth G	root C	third E
third E	fifth G	root E
root C	third E	fifth G
I	I6	I⁶₄

These arrangements do not change the name of the chord since it remains a combination of *C, E,* and *G,* but the individual members of the chord may be in different positions. In Ex. 3-10 above, (a) is called the position of the fifth, since the fifth is highest; (b) the position of the root, since the

<hr>

[6] See Chapter 10 for explanation of *mf* and other marks of expression.

root is highest; and (c) the position of the third, since the third is highest.

A further observation is that the root, third, or fifth of the chord may occur as the lowest tone of the chord. The Roman numeral standing alone, as at *a* above, indicates that the lowest tone of the chord is the root. This is known as the fundamental position. The figure six used in connection with the Roman numeral, as at *b,* indicates that the root of the chord is found six staff degrees above the lowest tone of the chord.[7] When this is true, the third (*E*) is the lowest tone of the chord. This last arrangement of tones is known as the first *inversion* of a triad. (Inversions will be discussed later.) The use of the six and four with the Roman numeral, as at *c,* indicates that the third (*E*) and the root (*C*) are respectively six and four staff degrees above the lowest tone of the chord. This arrangement leaves the fifth (*G*) as the lowest tone of the chord, and is known as the second inversion of a triad.

In like manner, a triad may be built on each tone of the scale, examples of which will be introduced as needed in subsequent chapters. The student should keep in mind two objectives in the study of each chord:

1. the ability to hear, sing, and write the members of a chord;
2. the ability to hear the total effect of a chord as it is played, especially during the singing of some of the melodies. As an initial experience in those respects, write Ex. 3-10 in the keys of G and D; play, listening to
   a. the tone in the upper voice part (position),
   b. the tone in the lower voice part,
   c. the tone in the middle,
   d. the total effect.

The tonic chord is the central chord of our tonal system, and nearly all compositions begin and end on some member of it.

Passing and neighboring tones. When a melody moves along the scale line from one member of a chord to another, the intervening *nonharmonic* tones (those not belonging to the chord) are known as *passing tones.* Although found with great frequency on the unaccented part of the measure, they also may occur on the accented tones. The same nonharmonic tones may occur as *neighboring tones* or a *turning tone.* This occurs when the melody progresses from a chord member to an adjoining degree (above or below) and returns to its original position. Both passing and neighboring tones may occur in any voice part, and in more than one voice at the same time. The passing and neighboring tones of the tonic chord are represented below by the black notes.

[7] In counting staff degrees, the student should be cautioned that the numbering is inclusive; that is, it begins with *E* and ends with *C:* E F G A B C
                                             1 2 3 4 5 6

Ex. 3–11

(a) Passing Tones of the Tonic Chord in *C*

(b) Neighboring Tones of the Tonic Chord in *C*

Distribution of chord tones. Since a triad contains only three tones, it is necessary in four part harmony to double one of the chord members thus supplying a voice part for soprano, alto, tenor, and bass. The doubling may be at the unison, or at one or more octaves. Of utmost importance for balance and aural effectiveness is the distribution of the triad tones. The arrangement may result in either *close* or *open* structure as illustrated below with the root of the chord in the bass. When the distance between the tenor and soprano is *not greater than the octave,* the chord is in *close* structure. The chord is in *open* structure when the distance between these two voices is *greater than the octave.*

Ex. 3–12

Write the chords above in the key of D; play them, listening carefully to each individual chord member and to the total effect.

Play and analyze[8] the harmonization of melody no. 9 from Melodies for Singing as shown below.

1. Note the close and open structure of the tonic chord.
2. Observe the passing and neighboring tones identified by the letters *P* and *N*.
3. Listen carefully to the total effect produced by the distribution of the tones of the triad.
4. Sing, directing aural attention to the various voice parts.

Ex. 3-13

The phrase. A single tone or chord, regardless of its beauty, has far less significance than a succession of related tones or chords; these produce values in thought and feeling inexpressible by a single tone or single chord. In music that we call beautiful, such successions are organized logically and effectively. Two of these are the *motive* and the *phrase.* The motive is the smallest of music ideas and is the germinal thought of a composition. This small melodic fragment of a musical theme or subject is often distinguishable by slight interruptions analogous to commas in a sentence within the phrase. The motive is often repeated exactly or in modification in developing logical coherence. A phrase may be defined as a musical idea possessing a certain degree of completion. It is usually, though not always, four measures in length. All music should be thought of in terms of these groups. Motives and phrases may be observed in Melodies for Singing.

8 Students with a piano background will find it valuable to transpose at the keyboard the harmonized examples found in each chapter.

Aids to reading music. By this time, the student undoubtedly has made a few observations which will aid him in reading music at sight. They may be summed up as follows:

1. If do (1) is on a line, mi (3), so (5), and ti (7) are on the lines above.
2. If do (1) is in a space, mi (3), so (5), and ti (7) are in the spaces above.
3. If do (1) is on a line, its octave above and below are in spaces.
4. If do (1) is in a space, its octave above and below are on lines.
5. In other words, do (1), mi (3), so (5), and ti (7) are always similarly placed either on lines or in spaces, whereas octaves are dissimilarly placed.

Rhythm

Quadruple meter and the divided beat. Some of the Melodies for Singing which follow are in quadruple meter. The conductor's beat pattern is shown below. Use it as *Holy, Holy, Holy* is played and sung.

Ex. 3-14

Holy, Holy, Holy

DYKES

Ex. 3-15

Quadruple Meter

Other Melodies for Singing contain examples of the divided beat. To understand and gain a feeling for this new rhythmic example, sing the first phrase of *Yankee Doodle,* observing the two notes to the beat.

Ex. 3-16

The metric signature indicates that there are two beats in each measure and that the quarter note will receive a beat; yet it is evident that there are twice as many notes in each of the first three measures as there are beats. This is due to the fact that the beat note (the quarter note) has been divided into two equal parts, which results in two notes for each beat. Use the conductor's beat as you sing *Yankee Doodle* again, observing this equal division of the beat note.

The counts for the two melodies above are indicated above the notes. There are several systems of counting, the one shown here being the old standard. Its plan is indicated below.

Ex. 3-17

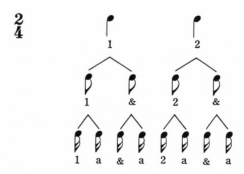

The student should use this or the system recommended by his instructor in connection with all Melodies for Singing.

Melodies for Singing and Dictation

The melodies in this chapter contain skips between the members of the tonic chord as well as the passing and neighboring tones. At times, other harmonies than the tonic may be implied, but our major attention must center upon the skips between the members of the tonic chord. This chord (when indicated by the Roman numeral I under the staff) should be played by the teacher or a member of the class as the melodies are sung. Concentrate upon hearing the skips between members of the chord, and the total aural effect when the tones are sounded simultaneously. Occasionally the student may notice a note in the melody which does not belong to the chord. Such a note may be a passing or neighboring tone.

Melodies for Singing

1. Andante — French Folk Song
2. Moderato — German Carol
3. Allegro — English Folk Song
4. Allegro — French Melody

⁹ See p. 171 for explanation for repeat dots.

Melodies for Dictation

11 See p. 60 for explanation of this key signature.

13 Adagio — Long, Long Ago — BAYLY

14 Adagio — Evening Prayer — From Hansel and Gretel — HUMPERDINCK

Suggestions for Further Study

Sing the Melodies for Singing again in the following manner: with one continuous sweep of the eye try to perceive an entire phrase. Close your eyes; visualize it; sing it mentally; then sing it aloud.

Write the Melodies for Dictation in quadruple meter in $\frac{4}{2}$ and $\frac{4}{8}$.

Identify the passing and neighboring tones of the tonic chord in the Melodies for Singing and Dictation. Find examples of these passing tones in music familiar to you.

Add the upper tetrachord to the lower tetrachords in Sec. (a) of the work sheet which follows, and write in the necessary sharps. Use the piano keyboard in working out the whole and half steps. After writing the scale, place the sharps in the key signature to the right of the additional clef provided and indicate the position of do (1), mi (3), and so (5). For proper placement of the sharps in the key signature, see p. 60. Play and sing each scale slowly. Play do (1), mi (3), and so (5) slowly in successive order, and then simultaneously, listening to the total effect.

Write, play, and sing the following melody in the keys of *G, D, A,* and *E* on the work sheet at (b):

Work Sheet

C (a)

do re mi fa so la ti do
1 2 3 4 5 6 7 8

do mi so do
1 3 5 8

36

C#

(b)

G

D

A

E

4

Major Scales and Keys

(Continued)

Rudiments

Other major scales. Once again sing the last phrase of *God of Our Fathers,* beginning this time on F². Now play the phrase, using white keys. The error occurred between 4 and 5 of the scale, and may be corrected by playing the black key to the left of B. This correction provides the whole step between 4 and 5 of the scale as well as the half step between 3 and 4. Compare the intervals of this scale with the scale formula presented in Chapter 3.

In order to represent the new black key on the staff it is necessary to place a character called a *flat* (♭) on B. When this symbol is placed on a degree of the staff, it causes that degree to represent a pitch one half step lower. The new scale appears on the staff and the keyboard in Ex. 4-1.

Ex. 4-1

Since the *B* flat is essential to the new scale, it becomes an integral part of the key of *F* and is, therefore, a diatonic tone. When music is written in this key, the flat is placed on the third line of the treble staff and on the second line of the bass staff, to the right of the clef. This is the sign of the key of *F;* and as the key signature, it indicates that each *B* on the staff is to be lowered one half step to *B* flat. The scale appears on both the treble and bass staffs in Ex. 4-2.

Ex. 4-2

f	g	a	b♭	c	d	e	f				
do	re	mi	fa	so	la	ti	do	do	mi	so	do
1	2	3	4	5	6	7	8	1	3	5	8

The student may have observed that the procedure in building this scale is a reversal of that used in the preceding chapter. Instead of counting *up* five degrees to find the key tone as was done in Chapter 3, we now count *down* five degrees to find the key tone of the new scale. It may also be observed that the lower tetrachord of the scale of *C* becomes the upper tetrachord of the scale of *F,* a phenomenon the opposite of that for the scales where sharps were employed. It may be noted further that the key of *F* has the very same tones as the key of *C,* with the exception of *B* flat; one reason the key of *F* is said to be related to the key of *C.*

Now let us take the lower tetrachord of the scale of *F* for the upper tetrachord of another new scale, the scale of *B* flat. Again we find it necessary to place a flat on the fourth degree of the new scale. The staff and keyboard representation of this new scale is shown in Ex. 4-3.

Ex. 4-3

The flats (*B* flat and *E* flat) are now placed on the third line and the fourth space of the staff (second line and third space in the bass) to form the key signature of the key of *B* flat major. (See Ex. 4-4.)

Ex. 4-4

The student should familiarize himself with these and other major flat key signatures. These are shown on p. 60. He should note the order of flats in the key signature carefully. As a guide to the identification of the keys employing flats, observe the following fact: since the last flat in the key signature is fa (4), count down four degrees to find do (1). If there is more than one flat in the key signature, do (1) will be on the same degree as the flat preceding the last one in the signature.[1]

Harmony

The dominant chord. As an introduction to the tones of the new chord we shall now consider, sing the following well-known melody:

Ex. 4-5

In the sixth measure (bracketed) we discover a tonal pattern new to us, the tones of the *dominant* chord. The dominant chord is built on the fifth tone of the scale, which in the key of *G* is *D*. Spelling this chord from the root with alternate letters or adjacent spaces, we find its members to be *D*, *F♯* and *A*. In example 4-5 the melody skips from the root up to the fifth and down to the third. The dominant chord is so named because the fifth tone of the scale and the chord built upon it have a dominating influence.

[1] See p. 60.

This chord, which in importance is second only to the tonic, is identified by the Roman V. It is shown below as it appears in the key of *C:*

Ex. 4-6

(a) Position of the fifth, the fifth being highest

(b) Position of the root, the root being highest

(c) Position of the third, the third being highest

(a) Fundamental position, the root being lowest

(b) First inversion, the third being lowest

(c) Second inversion, the fifth being lowest

The dominant chord is also important for the part it plays in the formation of phrases. We learned in Chapter 3 that a phrase is usually four measures in length and that it possesses a certain degree of completion.[2] It can now be added that each phrase ends with a cadence, a term meaning a close or fall which conveys the impression of a temporary or permanent conclusion. The type of cadence is determined by the choice of chord or chords coming at its close. When the phrase ends on the dominant chord, the cadence is known as the *half cadence* or close. When it ends on the tonic chord, preceded by the dominant triad, the close is known as an *authentic cadence*. The student must become increasingly conscious of phrases and the chord or chords which mark their endings. The Melodies for Singing found in this chapter contain examples of the half and authentic cadences.

Passing and neighboring tones in relation to the members of the dominant chord are shown in Ex. 4-7.

Ex. 4-7

(a) Passing Tones

(b) Neighboring Tones

Chord progression. Changing from one chord to another is known as *chord progression.* In doing this, the movement of each voice part and its relationship to the movement of other voices must be considered. Although not always possible in actual writing, the conventional progressions shown

[2] Phrases vary in length. The four measure phrase is found more frequently. However, the first phrase of "Come Thou Almighty King" (Ex. 2-2) is three measures long while the first phrase of "America" (Ex. 4-13) is six measures in length.

below are valuable for initial attempts in writing and playing as well as for basic harmonic hearing. In the conventional progressions, the tone that is common to both chords is retained in the same voice part while the remaining voices move to the nearest tones of the following chord. Such progressions from the tonic (I) to the dominant (V) are shown below in the keys of C and B flat. Observe the following:

1. The tonic chord in the key of C is C, E, G; the dominant chord is G, B, D; G is the common tone; it is retained in the same voice part. Observe further that regardless of the position of the tonic chord, the voices move in the same manner to the nearest tones of the dominant chord: G, G, G; E, D, E; C, B, C.

2. The tonic chord in the key of B flat is B flat, D, F; the dominant chord is F, A, C; F is the common tone; it is retained in the same voice part. Also note that the voices move in the same manner from the tonic to the dominant: F, F, F; D, C, D; B flat, A, B flat.

Chords for keyboard and harmonic ear training.

Ex. 4-8 (a)

Ex. 4-8 (b)

Play and write the progressions above in several keys, listening to the individual voice movements as well as the total effect of each chord, and the change of harmony. Playing the progression at (a) is made easy by moving the thumb and third fingers from C and E to the thumb and second finger of B and D. G, being the common tone, remains stationary under the little finger. Forming such finger habits makes the progression easy to play in any key. The finger movement from the other chord positions at (b) and (c) are likewise simple.

The chord progressions in Ex. 4-8 may be put to practical use by chording to some of the Melodies for Singing. In doing this, it is necessary to listen for the chord implied in the melody, and play the chord "by ear." You may use any one of the progressions ((a), (b), or (c)) in Ex. 4-8. The example below is melody No. 5 from Melodies for Singing.

Ex. 4–9

Or you may play the melody in the right hand and the chords in the left, using the progressions at (a) in Ex. 4-8 but in the key of G. Note the use of the V_6 chord in Ex. 4-10, paying particular attention to its over-all sound.

Ex. 4–10

Play and analyze the harmonization of melody No. 4 from Melodies for Singing, making the following observations:

(a) Tonic (I) chord in the key of F is F, A, C; dominant (V) chord is C, E, G.

(b) Observe the chord structure (open and close) and the passing tones.

(c) Listen to the total effect produced by the distribution of the triad tones.

(d) Note the half and authentic cadences.

(e) Observe the I_6 and V_6 (first inversions), and that the note in the soprano is doubled, which is the usual practice.

(f) Sing, listening to individual voices and to the total effect.

(g) Find examples where the common tone is not retained in the same voice part.

Ex. 4-11

French Folk Song

Rhythm

The tie and dot. For a new experience in rhythm, sing the melody in Ex. 4-12.

Ex. 4-12

Moderato

My coun - try 'tis - of thee, Sweet land of

---

[3] This tone belongs to the dominant seventh chord which will be considered in Chapter 6.

lib - er - ty, Of thee I sing.

It may be noted in this selection that the first note in the second and fourth measures is held for a beat and one-half, and that the second eighth note is sung as the last half of count two. Furthermore, the first eighth note in each case is not articulated, the pitch of the quarter note being prolonged through the durational value of both the quarter and the eighth. The symbol indicating this prolongation is a curved line called the *tie*. The tie welds two or more successive notes of the same pitch into a single sound equal to the combined durations of the notes so tied. As may be observed, only the first of the connected or tied notes is articulated, the second continuing automatically through the total time value of all notes concerned. The tie is particularly useful in combining into a single duration two notes which are separated by the measure bar.

Another way of indicating extended duration of tones is by the dot, which may be illustrated by a repetition of the same passage. (See Ex. 4-13.)

Here the *dot* in measures two and four has replaced the tie. As explained in Chapter 1, p. 7, a dot to the right of a note increases the time value of the note by one-half. Thus the time value of the dotted quarter in Ex. 4-13 is that of a quarter plus an eighth note. This, of course, consists of the same time value represented by the tie in Ex. 4-12, as may be seen by comparing the two. A further example of the use of the dot may be found in the last note of the passage. Here the value of the dot is that

Ex. 4-13

My coun - try 'tis of thee, Sweet land of

lib - er - ty, Of thee I sing

of a quarter, or one-half the value of the half note. Thus, the time value of the dotted half note here is that of three quarter notes. These could also be indicated by the tie in either of the following manners:

or

Melodies for Singing and Dictation

The melodies which follow contain examples of the skips between members of the tonic and dominant chords and of the dot. The I and V chords should be played on the piano as indicated in the melodies.

Melodies for Singing

Chorus of Shepherds   SCHUBERT

Come Unto These Yellow Sands   MARTINI

Love Songs   Waltz No. 9   BRAHMS

From Symphony No. 9   BEETHOVEN

13 Allegro moderato

English Melody

14 Allegro moderato

German Folk Melody, Arr. BRAHMS

15 Allegro

Waltz, Op. 156 No. 4   WALDTEUFEL

16 Allegro

Swabian Melody

17 Moderato

See the Conquering Hero Comes   From Judas Maccabeus   HANDEL

50

18 Andante

German Melody, Arr. BRAHMS

19 Moderato

Impromptus, Op. 142 No. 2   SCHUBERT

20 Andante

French Folk Song

Melodies for Dictation

1 Allegro

Arr. BRAHMS

11 Andante — French Folk Song

12 Allegro — From Symphony No. 9   BEETHOVEN

13 Andante — German Melody, Arr. BRAHMS

14 Moderato — Sandman's Song   from Hansel and Gretel   HUMPERDINCK

15 Andante — DYKES

16 Andante — American Melody

17 Adagio

Sanctus, Mass in G   MOZART

18 Moderato — Impromptu, Op. 142 No. 2   SCHUBERT

19 Allegro — English Folk Song

Suggestions for Further Study

Sing the Melodies for Singing again in the following manner: with one continuous sweep of the eye try to perceive an entire phrase. Close your eyes; visualize it; sing it mentally; then sing it aloud.

Examine several of your favorite compositions for examples of the dot.

Add the upper tetrachord to the lower tetrachord in Sec. (a) of the work sheet which follows, and write in the necessary flats. Use the piano keyboard in working out the whole and half steps. After writing the scale, place the flats in the key signature to the right of the clef provided and indicate the position of do (1), mi (3), and so (5). For proper placement of the flats in the key signature, see p. 60. Play and sing each scale slowly. Play do (1), mi (3), and so (5) slowly in successive order, and then simultaneously, listening to the total effect.

Write the dominant chord in the position of the fifth in the keys given in Sec. (b) of the work sheet.

Examine the Melodies for Singing above and other folk songs with which you are familiar for examples of motives, and for half and authentic cadences.

Work Sheet

55

(b)

5

Review of
Major Scales

Rudiments

The circle of fifths.   If the student has followed the tetra-
chordal system in writing the major scales as presented and assigned for
writing in Chapters 3 and 4, he has discovered fifteen key tones from which
scales may be built. It will be recalled that the upper tetrachord became the
lower tetrachord of each succeeding scale requiring an additional sharp.
Using this pattern, we discovered the following key tones, *C, G, D, A,
E, B, F♯,* and *C♯,* each of which was found to be five staff degrees up
from the preceding one. These key tones were assigned as part of the
Work Sheet in Chapter 3. The use of *F♯* and *C♯* (instead of *F* and *C*)
as key tones may seem surprising. Yet if we re-examine the upper tetrachords of the scales assigned for writing in Chapter 3, it will be noted that
F♯ and *C♯* were the beginning tones of the upper tetrachords of the B and
F♯ scales respectively. Further proof exists of the necessity for these
sharped degrees in the fact that an equal number of half steps (7) exists
between any key tone and the one immediately following, that is, *C* to *G,
G* to *D,* and so on. In addition, we have already learned from our study of
chords that the interval from *C to G* is a fifth, embracing as it does five
degrees of the staff. Five staff degrees are also involved in the intervals of
G to D, D to A, A to E, E to B, B to F♯, and *F♯ to C♯* as well as seven half
steps. These fifths, as will be learned in Chapter 11, are *perfect fifths.*

Turning now to review the scales employing flats, we will recall that the
lower tetrachord of a scale became the upper tetrachord in a succession of
scales having an additional flat. Consequently, the following key tones,
C, F, B♭, E♭, A♭, D♭, G♭, and *C♭* each of which was five staff degrees

down from the preceding one, were presented in the Work Sheet of Chapter 4. The necessity of having these flatted degrees as key tones is that each succeeding key tone is a perfect fifth below the preceding one.

The series of fifteen key tones (*C* being common) just discussed may be arranged in a circle showing the succession of fifths from one key tone to the next, a figure which is known as the *circle of fifths,* which is shown on page 60 with the key signatures in treble and bass.

The student must keep in mind the relationship existing between a given scale and its *attendant scales.* By attendant scales we mean those that immediately precede and follow a given scale. This is more easily understood when we recall that the tetrachords of a scale are also found in the two scales most closely related. For example, C is the given scale in Ex. 5-1; its upper tetrachord is the lower tetrachord of the G scale; its lower tetrachord is the upper tetrachord of F. Scale or key relationship, then, is based on the number of tones common to the scales under consideration, attendant scale differing by only one accidental from a given scale.

Ex. 5-1

Repetition and contrast.   In singing the melodies in previous chapters, the student may have already observed certain repetitions of motives and phrases. Repeated at the same pitch, such musical ideas are known as *exact repetition;* re-stated at a higher or lower pitch, they are known as a *sequence.* In some cases, there were slight tonal and rhythmic variations. As the essence of repetition, these uses are of great importance in giving unity to a melody. As a re-examination of the melodies already studied will reveal, such repetition is extensively used. For example, observe the use of repetition in Melody No. 1, p. 31.

In singing previous melodies, the student may also have observed new melodic ideas which, because of their rhythm and intervals, did not violate the basic unity of the melody. This skillful use of new but related materials illustrates the principle of contrast and serves the purpose of giving variety to music. For examples of the use of contrast, the student should examine the following: No. 17, p. 50, and No. 7, p. 67.

To summarize what has just been said, it may be stated that unity is achieved through repetition, and variety through contrast. It is through the combined use of these principles that the composer develops continuity and balance.

Enharmonic Keys [1]

[1] Enharmonic tones have the same pitch but different letter names.

Harmony

The subdominant chord.   Sing the following familiar melody:

Ex. 5–3

Be - lieve   me, if   all   those   en - dear - ing   young

Irish Melody

charms Which I   gaze   on so   fond - ly to - day_____

An unfamiliar tonal pattern appears in the second measure of this melody (bracketed), the skips between the chord tones of the *subdominant* or *underdominant* chord (IV). As may be observed, the chord originates on the fourth tone of the scale, and the other members are found in adjacent spaces. Its three positions, as it occurs in the key of *C*, are as follows:

Ex. 5–4

(a) Position of the fifth, the fifth being highest

C fifth
A third
F root

IV
(a) Fundamental position, the root being lowest

(b) Position of the root, the root being highest

F root
C fifth
A third

IV₆
(b) First inversion, the third being lowest

(c) Position of the third, the third being highest

A third
F root
C fifth

IV⁶₄
(c) Second inversion, the fifth being lowest

It is sometimes held that the subdominant is so named because it is under the dominant in the ascending scale. Actually, as shown in Ex. 5-5, it is so called because the subdominant (IV) is found a fifth below the tonic (I), whereas the dominant (V) is found a fifth above the tonic. In other words, IV is an underdominant of the tonic. Hence the prefix *sub* or *under*.

The tonic, dominant, and subdominant chords are known as the *principal triads* of a key, and, as shown in Ex. 5-5, their combined tones are those found in the major diatonic scale.

Ex. 5–5

IV   I   V

The passing and neighboring tones of the subdominant chord are shown in Ex. 5-6.

Ex. 5-6

(a)   Passing Tones

(b)   Neighboring Tones

The conventional progressions of the I, IV, and V chords are shown below in the keys of C and D. Like any chord progressions with fixed voice movement, they are easy to play in any key by establishing finger habits. Play and sing them slowly and thoughtfully:

(a) Listen to individual voices.

(b) Listen to the total effect or chord quality.

(c) Observe the common tone between I and IV, and between V and I. The common tone between I and IV in the key of C is C: *C*, E, G; F, A, *C;* in the key of D, it is D: *D*, F♯, A; G, B, *D*.

(d) There is no common tone between the IV and V chords. In such cases, the general rule is contrary motion. Observe, then, that in the progressions from IV to V the bass moves up and the remaining voices move down to the nearest tones of the dominant chord.

(e) Play and write these progressions in several keys.

Chords for keyboard and harmonic ear training.

Ex. 5-7 (a)

Ex. 5-7 (b)

Since the I, IV, and V chords contain the tones of the major scale, they may be used for chording in most folk songs and very simple melodies. In doing this, let the melody dictate the necessary chord change. Melody No. 12 from Melodies for Singing is used as an example.

Ex. 5-8

Now play the melody in the right hand (or sing it) and chords in the left. Note the use of the V_6 and the IV $\frac{6}{4}$.

Ex. 5-9

Austrian Folk Song

Melody No. 11 from Melodies for Singing is harmonized below for analysis and observation. Can you find an example of an accented passing tone, contrary motion, or where the common tone has not been kept in the same voice part?

Ex. 5-10

Rhythm

The tie and the slur. The tie was defined and explained in the preceding chapter in connection with the dot. Further examples of it follow in the Melodies for Singing. These should be noted carefully as the melodies are sung. The same symbol, a curved line, used for the tie is also used for the slur.[2] In its capacity as a slur, the line is used to connect consecutive notes representing different pitches. In its use in instrumental music (to be considered more fully in a later chapter), it means that the notes concerned are to be performed smoothly. In vocal music, it indicates that the tones so joined are to be sung to one word or syllable.

Melodies for Singing and Dictation

The following melodies contain examples of the chord tones of the subdominant chord, as well as of the dot, tie, and slur:

Melodies for Singing

Prayer of Thanksgiving   Dutch

---

[2] Although the slur is not a rhythmic device, it is introduced here in connection with the tie, since the same symbol is used for both.

Air de Ballet, Alceste   GLUCK

Duke Street   HATTON

Somerset Folk Song

5 Allegro

From the Magic Flute   MOZART

6 Allegro

There's Music in The Air   ROOT

7 Moderato

With a Painted Ribbon   BEETHOVEN

8 Largo   From Symphony No. 1   BRAHMS

9 Andante

O Shining Sun   SCHUMANN

10 Moderato   English Folk Song

11 Moderato

Hawaiian Folk Song

12 Andante

68

Austrian Folk Song

IV   I   I₆ IV I₆ V   I

13 Andante   American Indian Melody

14 Allegro

We're called _____ Gon - do - lier - i, but that's a va -

ga - ry, it's quite hon - or - a ry the trade that we ply _____

We're Called Gondolieri   From The Gondoliers   SULLIVAN

15 Moderato

How love - ly is ____ thy dwell - ing place, o

How Lovely Is Thy Dwelling Place   BRAHMS

Lord _____ of hosts, o Lord of hosts

16 Allegro

The_ first_ No - el the_ an - gels did say Was to
They_ look - ed up and_ saw_ a star Shin - ing

cer - tain poor shep-herds in fields as they lay; In _ fields_ where
in ____ the East _ be - yond_ them far, And_ to ____ the

they lay_ keep-ing their sheep On a cold win-ter's night_ that
earth it_ gave_ great light And_ so it con - tin - ued both

69

was — so deep. No - el, No - el, No - el, No-
day — and night.

The First Noel, Traditional

el, Born is the King — of Is - ra - el

17 Andante
mf
3

My Sun   DI CAPUA
3

18 Allegro
f
Christ the Lord is ris'n to-day — Al - - le - lu - ia
I   V6 I   IV6 IV I   I⁶₄ V I

Christ The Lord Is Ris'n Today.   From DAVIDICA
Sons of men and an - gels say: — Al - - le - lu - ia
IV6 I   IV I6   I⁶₄ V   I⁶₄ V I

Melodies for Dictation

1 Allegro   Somerset Folk Song
f

2 Allegro   English Folk Song
mf

³ See p. 144 for explanation of the triplet.

Suggestions for Further Study

Write from memory the key signatures in bass and treble at (a) on the work sheet.

Identify the key signatures of several of your favorite compositions. Also look for examples of the dot, tie, and slur.

Write the I, IV, and V chords, position of the fifth, in the keys of C, G, D, A, F, Bb, Eb, Ab on the work sheet at (b). Play them for total effect.

Note the phrases ending on the tonic and dominant chords and the use of the V to I progression in the final cadence of the above Melodies for Singing.

Examine the melodies in this and preceding chapters for examples of repetition and contrast.

Work Sheet

(a)

(b)

6

Tempo

Rudiments

Tempo indications. Tempo is an Italian word used to express the speed at which a composition is executed. Many of the terms used in the interpretation and expression of music come from the Italians, who were the first to make wide use of such designations. Prior to 1600, tempo marks were almost unknown, since the rate of speed was expressed by the notation itself; that is, the beat and note values had absolute duration, only slight variations in speed being possible. But with the introduction of special words to denote tempo, a wide variety of speeds were made possible. Terms from other languages may also be found in music, since many composers prefer the use of their native tongues. In addition to words, or in conjunction with them, the composer may also use readings from an instrument called the *metronome* to indicate different rates of speed.

The metronome, by means of an inverted, swinging pendulum, the speed of which is controlled by a sliding weight, produces a set number of clicks per minute. If the pendulum weight, for example, is set at 60, the metronome will give sixty clicks per minute, each click representing a beat. In designating metronome speed, the composer uses a formula: M.M. ♩ = 60, or M.M. ♩ = 60, or M.M. ♪ = 60. The letters M.M. signify Maelzel's metronome—named after Maelzel, its inventor. In slow tempos of compound meter such as $\frac{6}{8}$ $\frac{9}{8}$ $\frac{12}{8}$ the composer uses the eighth note in his metronomic markings, and in fast tempos the dotted quarter: for example, M.M. ♪ = 72, M.M. ♩. = 72. By the use of metronomic formulas, the composer is able to indicate precisely the rate of speed at which he wishes his composition to move.

The more recent electric metronomes are superior to Maelzel's for the reason that they are absolutely accurate and easier to manipulate. No winding or setting of a sliding weight is necessary; the instrument is simply plugged into an electric outlet and the dial set at the speed desired. Moreover, the speed may be changed without stopping the instrument by merely turning the dial. Some of the electrical metronomes use a click to indicate the beat, others a flash of light.

Before the invention of the metronome, the composer could not provide a definite indication of tempo; he could only use words to express in a general way what his wishes were in regard to speed. The most common of these terms, already given in Chapter 2, may be repeated for review.

Grave—slow and solemn	Andante—going, moving at
Lento—slow	moderate rate
Largo—large, broad, slow	Allegro—cheerful, quick
Adagio—at ease, leisurely	Vivace—very lively
Moderato—in moderate tempo	Presto—very, very lively

Most of the words given above may be modified by the endings *etto* and *ino,* which diminish, or *issimo,* which increases the effect of the word so modified. Thus *allegretto* indicates a tempo somewhat slower than allegro, and *allegrissimo* a more rapid speed than allegro. Sometimes phrases which have historically identified traditional musical forms, such as *tempo di minuette* (in the time of the minuet), are used to indicate tempo. The words listed above are also combined sometimes with one another, and with other words. Although to list and define these combinations is not the object of this textbook, certain of them should become familiar to the student. Study the following miscellaneous words and phrases:

A—at, for, with	Molto—much
Animato—animated	Non—not
A poco a poco—little by little	Piu—more
Assai—very	Poco—a little
Ben—well	Quasi—almost
Ben marcato—well marked	Risoluto—in a resolute manner
Cantabile—in a singing style	Rubato—robbed time—increasing
Con—with	and decreasing tempo in a pas-
Con moto—with motion	sage
Con spirito—with spirit	Simplice—simply
Farza—force or emphasis	Sempre—always
Grandioso—grandly	Simile—in the same manner
Grazioso—gracefully	Sostenuto—sustained
Ma—but	Sotto voce—in a subdued manner
Marcato—marked	Tranquillo—tranquilly
Meno—less	Troppo—too, too much
Mezzo—half	Vigoroso—vigorously

If the composer wishes the tempo to be increased or decreased during the rendition of a composition in order to give variety and to make it more intelligible, he indicates these changes by such expressions as *ritardando* and *accelerando*. The most common of these terms, with the abbreviations by which they are sometimes indicated, are as follows:

Accelerando (accel.)—accelerating
Poco a poco animato—animated little by little
Ritardando (rit.) ⎫
Rallentando (rall.) ⎬—gradually retarding
A tempo—in the original tempo
Ad libitum (ab lib.)—at the performer's pleasure

As was indicated above, this list is incomplete, but it is sufficient to give the student a working knowledge of the terms used to indicate tempo. It is well to state here that some of the modern composers use English words to express their desires with regard to tempo and expression.

Perfect and imperfect authentic cadence. In Chapter 4 we learned that the dominant to tonic progression at the close of a phrase was known as the authentic cadence, so called because these chords establish the key. Such a close is said to be *perfect* when the melody ends on the key tone and *imperfect* when the melody ends on the third or fifth of the tonic chord. For example, a V-I progression (fundamental positions) with the key tone in the soprano produces a *perfect authentic cadence;* the same chord progression with the third or fifth of the tonic chord in the melody (or first inversion) produces the *imperfect authentic cadence.* It should be added that cadences usually are found on the accented part of the measure.

Harmony

The dominant seventh. Sing the following melody, observing the chord tones found in the bracketed measures:

Ex. 6-1

Tyrolese Folk Song

As may be observed, the skips are all on the dominant, plus an additional third above the fifth, or E, G♯, B, D. It will be remembered that a three-tone chord is called a triad and is built by adding a third and fifth on alternate staff degrees above the root. A four-tone chord, as in Ex. 6-1 above, built in a similar manner, is called a *seventh-chord,* since seven degrees of the staff are embraced between the root and the highest tone,

E, F♯, G♯, A, B, C♯, D. Since this chord of the seventh is built on the
1   2   3   4   5   6   7

dominant of the scale, it is called the dominant-seventh (V_7). It is often referred to as the seventh of the staff degree on which it originates, in the example above, the E; in other words, the E_7.

The dominant-seventh, like the dominant, is one of the most important chords in music and is often used as a substitute. When the four tones are sounded together, the total effect is that of anticipation or expectancy, a quality which results from the combination of active tones contained.[1] This combination of active tones is classified as *dissonant,* and its active or expectant tendency may be satisfied by moving to inactive tones. This movement of active tones of the dominant-seventh to the rest, or *consonant*[2] tones of the tonic, may be heard by playing the last two measures of Ex. 6-1 above. The dominant-seventh as it occurs in the key of C is shown below in its four positions:

Ex. 6-2

(a) Position of the 7th, the 7th being highest

F seventh
D fifth
B third
G root

V_7

(b) Position of the root, the root being highest

G root
F seventh
D fifth
B third

V_5^6

(c) Position of the 3rd, the 3rd being highest

B third
G root
F seventh
D fifth

V_3^4

(d) Position of the 5th, the 5th being highest

D fifth
B third
G root
F seventh

V_2^4

The student should observe the figures used in connection with the dominant-seventh as they are employed with all four-tone chords. At (b) the six and five identify the root (G) and seventh (F); at (c) the four and three designate the root (G) and seventh (F); and at (d) the four and two identify the third (B) and the root (G).

[1] See Chapter 3, p. 24.
[2] See Chapter 14, p. 200.

Ex. 6-3

Passing and Neighboring Tones
(Other than those given for the dominant)

The conventional progressions of the I, IV, V_7, and I are shown below in the keys of C and E flat; in addition to these, play them in B flat, D, A, and A flat. It will be observed that the fifth (D in the key of C, and F in the key of E flat) are missing in the progressions at (a) (b) and (c), and that the root is doubled. This is often the case with the V_7. At (d) is an example employing the fifth. Play the examples slowly:

(a) Observe the smooth voice movement and the common tones, especially the new one between IV and V_7.

(b) Listen to individual voices and the over-all effect.

Chords for keyboard and harmonic ear training.

Ex. 6-4

I   IV   V₇   I   I   IV   V₇   I

As stated earlier, the V_7 may be used instead of the V. This is certainly true in chording to melodies. Melody No. 4 from *Melodies for Singing* is used as an example.

Ex. 6–5

French Folk Song

I   I IV I   V₇   I   I IV I   V₇   I

Note the use of the IV $^6_4$ and the V $^6_5$ below.

Ex. 6–6

French Folk Song

I IV$^6_4$ I   V$^6_5$ I   I IV$^6_4$ I   V$^6_5$ I

Melody No. 13 from *Melodies for Singing* is harmonized below for analysis and observation.

Ex. 6–7

I   I₆   I   I₆   V   V₆   I

Rhythm

Compound duple meter. In the Melodies for Singing in previous chapters we have experienced duple, triple, and quadruple meters, all simple meters. We are now ready to consider a compound meter, the compound duple. The conductor's beat pattern for this meter is shown in Ex. 6-8.

Ex. 6-8

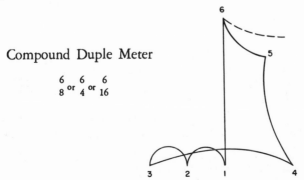

Compound Duple Meter

$$\frac{6}{8} \text{ or } \frac{6}{4} \text{ or } \frac{6}{16}$$

Using the conductor's pattern, sing Ex. 6-9. Since this is a relatively slow-moving melody, we are able to feel each beat or count individually, and in such cases the conductor usually indicates each beat according to the pattern shown in Ex. 6-8. As explained in Chapter 2, the beats are in groups of three (strong, weak, weak), with two groups in each measure, and an accent on the first of each group.

Ex. 6-9

In contrast to the slow tempo of Ex. 6-9, sing the following, using the conductor's pattern.

Ex. 6-10

At so rapid a pace, the student probably found it impossible to move his hand quickly enough to indicate individual beats. Yet the pulsations were definitely in groups of threes, and no doubt a tendency was felt to tap the foot at the beginning of each group where the accent is found. Now sing the melody again, using only two beats in each measure. Observe that the beat fell either on a dotted quarter, which is equivalent to three eighth notes, or at the beginning of groups of three eighth notes. We may conclude from this experience that the conductor employs only two beats to the measure[3] in rapid tempos of compound duple meter, and

---

[3] For the conductor's pattern for duple meter, see Chapter 2. For additional suggestions on the fundamentals of conducting, see Appendix.

that one beat is given to each dotted quarter note or its equivalent. Note that the metronomic marking in Ex. 6-10 indicates that the tempo is at 72 dotted quarter notes per minute. Rapid tempos in compound meters are sometimes indicated at the beginning of the music in this manner.

Melodies for Singing and Dictation

The following melodies contain examples of the melodic use of the tones of the dominant-seventh and examples in compound duple meter.

Melodies for Singing

5 Andante

I   I I₆ IV   I   IV   I

Russian Folk Song

V₇   I I₆ IV   I   V₇   I

6 Adagio

The Little Dustman   BRAHMS

7 Moderato

I   I   I   V   V₇

V₇   V   I I₆ IV   I₆

Cradle Song   BRAHMS

V₇   I I₆ IV   I   V₇ I⁶₄ V₇ I

8 Presto

I   I   V₇   I   I

Swedish Folk Song

9 Andante

If With All Your Hearts   From Elijah   MENDELSSOHN

10 Allegro

Dona Nobis   From Twelfth Mass   MOZART

11 Slow Waltz

Waltz Song   From The Merry Widow   LEHAR

12　Andante

Dutch Folk Song

13　Andante

French Folk Song

14　Andante

French Folk Song

84

I'm Going Away   BRAHMS

20   Allegretto grazioso (♩.= 116)

Fugue From Well Tempered Clavichord   BACH

Melodies for Dictation

1   Presto   Old Song

2   Moderato   Tyrolese Folk Song

3   Presto   Swedish Folk Song

4   Moderato   Russian Folk Song

5   Allegretto   SUSSMAYER

6   Allegro   Welsh Melody

7   Moderato   Our Country   HAYDN

87

19 Allegro   Careless, Idle Maiden   From Faust   GOUNOD

Suggestions for Further Study

Observe the tempos of several compositions from the classical and modern periods.

Write the dominant-seventh chord in all major keys on the work sheet. Play them, and listen to the total effect and expectant tendency of this combination of active tones.

Identify the half and authentic cadences in the above Melodies for Singing.
Find examples of the perfect authentic cadences in the above melodies.

Examine the following imperfect cadences: No. 17, p. 121 (dictation); No. 14, p. 135; No. 11, p. 147; No. 3, p. 159; No. 5, p. 175.

Work Sheet

7

The Minor Scale

Rudiments

The major and minor mode.   Play and sing the following familiar melody:

Ex. 7-1

The contrast between *A* and *B* above results from the use of two different *modes, A* being in the *minor mode,* seeming to have *E* as its key center, and *B* being in the *major mode,* tending to center around *G.* The contrast is, further, the result of the use of a different order of whole and half steps (to be treated more fully in Chapter 8) employed in the scales belonging to each of the modes. It should be noted that the key signature remains the same for both modes.

We have been using the term *mode* in its specific musical sense; it also has the more general meaning of *style* or *manner.* In a sense, this broader meaning also applies to the example above; that is, *A* seems to be in one manner or style and *B* in another. In our further discussions, however, the term will be used in its specific sense as defined above.

These two modes are used in music today for historical reasons. Because of their original association and the confusion over key signatures, the relationship of the two modes has been a controversial subject. There are basic facts concerning the two modes, however, on which all theorists agree. These facts and theories will be treated in this and in the following chapter.

The relative minor scale. For further observations concerning the modes, let us construct a scale from the key centers of the *A* and *B* parts of Example 7-1 above.

Ex. 7-2

It will be noted that these two scales have a common signature and employ the same tones; the scales, however, begin at a different place and on a different key tone—which means, of course, that they are different keys, the first called *E* minor and the second *G* major. When this is true of major and minor scales, they are said to be relative.[1] *E* minor is said to be the relative minor of *G* major, and *G* major, the relative major of *E* minor. Two further observations may be made: (1) that the key center for the minor is found three degrees, comprising three half steps, below the major key center, and conversely, the key center for the major is found three degrees, comprising three half steps, above the minor key center; (2) that the name of the major key is the same as the third tone of the minor scale.

Now let us construct these scales in the same setting as they originally appeared historically. The student should note that they also have a com-

[1] Theorists differ as to the particular syllables used in singing the minor scale. Since this is true, the two possible sets of syllables are given here. Regardless of which set of syllables is used, the object is to hear and to sing the minor mode accurately. See the next chapter for justification for *do* as the key tone of the minor.

mon signature and employ the same tones, but begin on a different key tone, and that the minor scale begins three degrees and three half steps below the major.

Ex. 7-3

The minor scale, unlike the major, exists in a variety of forms. The historical form used above is known as the *modal, natural,* or *pure* form of the minor scale. Note, however, that it does not have a leading tone, or half step, between 7 and 8. In order to obtain one, and thus definitely strengthen the effect of the key tone, it is necessary to raise the pitch of the seventh step (G) one half tone to G♯. Note that this change makes the scale progressions 7-8 or 8-7 in *A* minor correspond to those in *A* major, thus:

Ex. 7-4

This is known as the *harmonic* form of the minor scale because it is the one most frequently used in harmony.

In order to avoid the awkward melodic interval resulting from this change—the step and a half now found between the sixth and seventh degrees—it is necessary in the ascending scale to raise the pitch of the sixth step (*F*) one half tone to F♯—thus making the upper tetrachord (5-6-7-8) identical with that of *A* major. However, in the descending scale the natural form of the minor scale is used (*A-G-F-E*) as in Ex. 7-3. These two variants are known as the *melodic* form of the minor scale. (See Ex. 7-5 on following page.)

The symbols used on G and F are known as *naturals.* Such a character is used to cancel a sharp or a flat and thus to restore a note to its staff pitch. In order to raise the sixth and seventh steps in some of the keys, it is necessary to use a double sharp (.×.) when the key signature designates a sharp on these degrees. The double sharp causes a degree on which a sharp has already been placed to represent a pitch one half step higher. A single sharp is used to restore a degree having a double sharp back to its staff pitch. On degrees which have been lowered by a flat in the key signature, it will be necessary to use the natural to cause them to represent a pitch one half step higher.

Ex. 7-5

la	ti	do	re	mi	fi	si	la		la	so	fa	mi	re	do	ti	la
1	2	3	4	5	6	7	8		8	7	6	5	4	3	2	1

To summarize, we have three forms of the minor scale: the *natural,* the *harmonic,* and the *melodic.* Of these, the harmonic is the most important, since it is the basis for construction of the principal chords in the minor key. Its lowered third and sixth become the third in the tonic and subdominant chords, and the raised seventh becomes the third of the dominant chord, as will be seen in the chapters which follow.

The period. The average eight measure melody seems to fall into two parts or phrases of four measures each, the two being closely related; the first phrase seems to ask a question, and the second to answer it. The two are called, respectively, the *antecedent* and the *consequent.* The end of the antecedent is usually marked by some member of the dominant chord, although the imperfect authentic cadence may be used instead. The consequent usually ends with the perfect authentic cadence, though it also may end with the imperfect authentic cadence. The particular arrangement of phrases suggested by the discussion above is called a *period,* and it is sometimes referred to as the complete musical sentence. The following melodies illustrate this form: No. 4, p. 31; No. 8, p. 48; No. 17, p. 50; No. 1, p. 81.

Harmony

The tonic chord in minor. We now turn to a consideration of the melodic use of the tones of the minor scale, and specifically to the tones of the chord founded on the first tone of the minor scale. Since the triad is built on the first tone, it is called the tonic chord. Like other triads, it

Ex. 7-6

(a) Position of the fifth, the fifth being highest

E fifth
C third
A root

I

(a) Fundamental position, the root being lowest

(b) Position of the root, the root being highest

A root
E fifth
C third

I₆

(b) First inversion, the third being lowest

(c) Position of the third, the third being highest

C third
A root
E fifth

I⁶₄

(c) Second inversion, the fifth being lowest

---

2 The student must not conclude from this presentation that the sixth and seventh are always raised in the ascending form and lowered in the descending. The upper tetrachord of the minor scale is variable, depending upon the harmonic background. See Melody No. 5, p. 101.

is constructed by adding a third and fifth above the root, using alternate letters of the staff. It is shown in Ex. 7-6 in the key of *A* minor in its three positions. As you play these tones together, note that the effect is different from that of the tonic chord in the major key; the reason is that the interval of the third of the tonic in minor is one half step smaller than that of the tonic in major. This will be explained more fully in Chapter 8. Play the example in E, D, C, and F minor, listening to

(a) the tone in the uppermost voice,
(b) the tone in the lowest voice,
(c) the tone in middle voice,
(d) the total effect.

Passing and neighboring tones of the tonic chord in *A* minor:

Ex. 7-7

Chordal accompaniment. Thus far, your keyboard experience has been limited to playing the chords in their simplest arrangement. Now that you are somewhat familiar with the chords and the fingering for progressions, chording may be made more interesting through rhythmic variety. This may be accomplished by playing chord members in both hands as the melody is sung, or by supplying the chords in the left hand while playing the melody in the right hand. There are no rules governing such chording but it is suggested that the lowest note of the chord occur on the accented part of the measure and that this note be either the root or third of the chord, the intervening responses being an inversion. The basic rhythmic examples below in two-four, four-four, three-four, and six-eight are by no means arbitrary, for there are many variants. Begin by selecting an appropriate rhythmic pattern for each of the melodies to which you have been chording in previous chapters; using the chosen rhythm play the progressions as in the past. Then try rhythmic chording to less familiar melodies. The examples below also apply to the minor keys, and to chords yet to be introduced.

Ex. 7-8

Ex. 7-9

Rhythm

The subdivided beat. For a new experience in rhythm, sing the
following melody, observing the use of the sixteenth notes (Ex. 7-10). It
is evident in this example that the quarter note (the note receiving the

beat) has been divided into eighths, and in some cases the eighths further divided into sixteenths. This may be seen by an examination of the first measure, from which it is apparent that the two eighth notes, as well as the four sixteenths, are performed during the time equivalent of one beat. The two sixteenths following the dotted quarter note in measures 5, 6, 7 (bracketed) are, of course, divisions of an eighth note and are performed in that time value. Sing the melody again, using the conductor's beat pattern, and observe the feeling produced by the groupings of sixteenth notes.

Ex. 7-10

Melodies for Singing and Dictation

The following melodies contain examples of the melodic use of chord tones of the tonic triad in minor and of the subdivided beat.

Melodies for Singing[3]

[3] For signatures of minor keys see Chapter 9, Ex. 9-1.

French Folk Song

7 Moderato

From Tannhäuser WAGNER

8 Andante

Russian Folk Song

9 Moderato

French Folk Song

10 Moderato

German Melody, Arr. BRAHMS

11 Allegro

Russian Folk Song

12 Allegro

French Folk Song

13 Moderato

Whither   SCHUBERT

14 Moderato

Folk Song   Arr. BRAHMS

15 Andante moderato   Jesu, Joy of Man's Desiring   BACH

16 Andante   My Heart Ever Faithful   BACH

100

Melodies for Dictation

Suggestions for Further Study

Write the relative minor scale of all major keys in bass and treble, using the three forms of the minor scale.[4] After writing the key signature of the major key, write the minor scale, beginning on the third degree below the major key tone. This gives the natural form. Now raise the seventh tone to give the harmonic form, and finally raise both the sixth and seventh to obtain the melodic form. In descending, use the natural form. Play and sing these scales many times as you carefully observe the positions of 1, 3, 5, and 8.

Write and sing the following melody in the keys of *E, G, B,* and *D* minor.

[4] See Chapter 9, p. 124.

Write the tonic chord in its three positions in the minor keys. Play them, listening to the total effect.

Work Sheet

Pure   Harmonic   Melodic

Pure   Harmonic   Melodic

E

8

The Minor Scale

(Continued)

Rudiments

The tonic minor scale.   Play the following example from the Beethoven Piano Sonata Op. 14, No. 2:

Ex. 8-1

The key signature for this passage is G, but our ears tell us that the mode is minor rather than major. Evidently, then, Beethoven has changed the mode without changing the key—simply by lowering the third of the scale (B) and the sixth (E). This may be clearer if we examine the following example:

Ex. 8-2

Both of these scales are constructed from G, but the first is the major and the second the minor scale. The change of mode was accomplished, then, by lowering the third and sixth degrees of the major scale by one half step. The result is the harmonic form of the minor scale. Had Beethoven desired the use of the pure form, he would have had to lower the seventh also. The three forms of the minor scale in G appear thus:

Ex. 8-3

Our comparison of structure indicates that the real difference between the major and the minor mode is that the minor third, sixth, and seventh are lower by one half step than they are in the major. As shown above, the lowering of the third, sixth, and seventh produces the natural form; the lowering of only the third and sixth, the harmonic; the lowering of the third, the melodic. The only consistent change here, of course, is the lowered third, since in minor the major form is often used for the upper portion or tetrachord of the scale. In other words, the upper portion of the scale is variable. Thus mode, or style or manner, refers more specifically to the interval pattern of the scale than to a change in key, as we shall see in a moment.

Had Beethoven desired to remain in the key of G minor for a considerable length of time, he would have placed the flats in the key signature instead of writing them in each time they were needed. If this plan were followed, our three forms would appear thus:

But whether the third, sixth, and seventh are lowered as needed or placed in the key signature, the key remains the same: in this case, G minor.

When the minor scale has the same tonic or key tone as the major, as in the Beethoven example, the scales are said to be *parallel*. Hence G minor is the parallel minor of G major and G major is the parallel major of G minor. Since the term *tonic* is sometimes applied to such scales because they have the same tonics, G minor is often called the tonic minor of G major, and conversely.

A review of the illustrations used in this and the preceding chapter suggests broadly the manner in which composers employ the major and minor modes. Whereas Part A of "We Three Kings" (see Ex. 7-1, p. 90) is in the key of E minor, Part B or the chorus is in the key of G major. This was possible under the same key signature since the two scales contained the same tones. In the Beethoven example (see Ex. 8-1, p. 107) however, where the major mode is changed to the minor, alterations of the scale steps were necessary, since these are not represented by the same key signature. In the use of the two modes, then, the composer has the following choices: (1) major key, (2) its relative minor, and (3) the parallel or tonic minor.

In order to lower the third, sixth, or seventh degrees when these have already been lowered by a flat in the key signature, it is necessary to use a double flat (♭♭) to effect a pitch one half step lower. To restore a degree where a double flat has been employed to its original single flat status, a single flat is used.

Parallel and contrasting construction of the period.   When the initial portion of the consequent phrases of a period is an exact repetition of the first part of the antecedent, a period is said to be in *parallel construction*. The student should study the following melodies as examples of periods in parallel construction: No. 4, p. 31; No. 10, p. 32; No. 8, p. 48; No. 10, p. 49; No. 15, p. 85; No. 4, p. 114; No. 1, p. 144; and No. 10, p. 49.

When the consequent phrase is melodically—and, sometimes, rhythmically—in contrast to the antecedent phrase, the period is in *contrasting construction*. The following melodies illustrate this: No. 17, p. 50; No. 1, p. 81; No. 16, p. 85; No. 12, p. 100; No. 15, p. 148; No. 3, p. 174.

The dominant chord in the minor key has for its root the fifth tone of the key. The third and fifth are added on alternate staff degrees in the key of *A* minor, as shown below:

Ex. 8-5

(a) Position of the 5th, the 5th being highest

(b) Position of the root, the root being highest

(c) Position of the 3rd, the 3rd being highest

(a) Fundamental position, the root being lowest .

(b) First inversion, the 3rd being lowest

(c) Second inversion, the 5th being lowest

Special attention must be called to the raised third of this chord. As was stated in Chapter 7, in harmony, the harmonic form of the minor scale is used. In this form, it will be recalled, the seventh tone of the scale is raised. Since in the key of *A* minor, G is the seventh tone of the scale, and is, of course, the third of the dominant chord, it must be raised. In fact, the dominant triad in the minor is the same as the dominant chord in the parallel major—that is, the chord is the same in *A* major and *A* minor.

Ex. 8-6

(a)

Passing Tones

(b)

Neighboring Tones

The conventional progressions of the I and V chords are shown below in the keys of A and D minor. Play them slowly and thoughtfully in the keys of E and F minors, keeping the following in mind:

(a) Observe the common tone
(b) Listen to the individual voice parts
(c) Listen to the over-all effect.

Observe how the I and V chords are employed in chording to melody No. 4 from Melodies for Singing.

Ex. 8-8

French Folk Song

Use the following pattern in the left hand while playing the melody in the right.

Ex. 8-9

Melody No. 1 from Melodies for Singing is harmonized below for observation and study. Notice the distribution of the voices, and the change of mode.

Ex. 8-10

Rhythm

For a new experience in rhythm, sing the following melody:

Ex. 8-11

March time   Battle Hymn of the Republic   STEFFE

Mine   eyes have seen the glo-ry of the com-ing of   the Lord

If we analyze this dotted-eighth-sixteenth rhythm, we find that the combined value of this combination of tones is equal to one quarter or one beat. By using the tie we can get a clearer picture of what actually takes place within the beat: ♪♪♪♪ . In other words, the dotted-eighth length contains three sixteenths, which leaves only one sixteenth for the final portion of the beat. Since the two notes come in the over-all time of a quarter note, they may be compared to two eighth notes. Eighth notes are equal divisions of the beat (and too often performed unequally), while the dotted-eighth—sixteenth is an unequal division. The rhythm may be felt best by thinking the sixteenth note very quickly just before the following beat.

Melodies for Singing and Dictation

The following melodies contain the melodic use of the dominant chord tones in minor, as well as examples of the dotted eighth-sixteenth rhythm.

Melodies for Singing

113

From Symphony No. 5   DVORAK

11 Allegro

Awake, My Soul   HANDEL

12 Andante

116

French Carol

13 Allegro

Morris Dance Tune

14 Moderato

German Melody   BRAHMS

15 Andante

Norwegian Folk Song

16 Moderato

Cradle Song   SCHUBERT

117

17 Allegro

f I(c)   V Major I   I Major   I V Major   I Minor
     (E)   (c)

I V I   I   I Major   V₇ Major   I Major
                (Eb)   Swedish Folk Song

V Major   I Minor   I   V   I   I⁶₄ V   I
     (c)

18 Allegro

mp

Song of the Bird Catcher   From The Magic Flute   MOZART

19 Moderato

p

Swedish Folk Song

20 Andante

Dearest Name From Rigoletto VERDI

Melodies for Dictation

1 Andante German Melody, Arr. BRAHMS

2 Andante English Melody

3 Andante Hungarian Melody

4 Moderato Love is Forever BRAHMS

5 Allegro From Symphony No. 5 DVORAK

6 Lento Nocturn Opus 15 No. 3 CHOPIN

Suggestions for Further Study

Convert each of the major scales into a minor by lowering the third, sixth, and seventh tones.

Write the tonic chord in the major keys; convert each to a minor tonic chord by lowering the third. Play the major and then the minor, listening to the contrasting effects.

Sing the melodies in minor keys found in Melodies for Singing again, noticing the apparent change of mode from minor to major, then from major to minor.

Examine several of your favorite compositions for examples of the three forms of the minor scale. Note the upper tetrachords, particularly the raised sixth and seventh in descending passages in No. 11 of the Bach Two-Part Inventions.

Work Sheet

9

Review of Major and Minor Keys

Rudiments

Relationship of scales, keys, and chords.   The key signature

Ex. 9-1

of all the major and minor keys and the tonic chord of each is given in Ex. 9-1. The student should become thoroughly familiar with each.

It was shown in Chapter 5 that the scales which immediately precede and follow a given scale are known as attendant or related scales, and that the scales of *F* and *G* major were closely related to that of *C* major. The relative minors, when they are added to *F, C,* and *G* major scales, are also in very close relation to the key of *C*. The attendant scales, with the more technical terms applied to such relationship, are shown below:

Ex. 9-2

The same relationship also exists between a given minor scale and its attendant scales, as shown in Ex. 9-3.

Ex. 9-3

So far our consideration of the relationship existing between scales, keys, and chords has not touched on the fundamental and significant reason for its existence. In Chapter 1 it was noted that the tones of the scale were related by natural laws of sound; in other words, they are based upon the physical fact that a vibrating body, such as a string, produces a series of sounds called *overtones* or *harmonics,* all of which exist in fixed ratio to the *fundamental tone* produced by the vibrating body.

Let us consider for a moment what happens when a string vibrates. Actually, it vibrates both as a whole and in segments. When such a string is touched at its midpoint, the two parts, being one-half as long, will vibrate twice as fast, producing a sound an octave above the pitch of the full length string. If the string is divided into three equal parts, the tone for each will be a twelfth above the original; if divided into four equal parts, the tone will be that of the double octave. And so on.

Example 9-4 shows great *C* as the fundamental and its accompanying overtones. In any instance in which the overtones are designated, the fundamental tone is called the first *partial;* the first overtone, or octave above the fundamental, the second partial, and the second overtone, the third partial, and so on. Note the numbering of partials in Ex. 9-4. The use of numbers provides a means of calculating the ratios of the partials to each other mathematically. For example, the vibratory ratio of the octave is 1:2 —that is, the vibrations of the upper tone of the octave are twice those of the lower; the ratio of the fifth is 2:3; etc.

Ex. 9-4

Two observations may be made. (1) The second overtone (*G*) stands in very close relationship to the fundamental (*C*) because it is the first pitch differing in letter from the fundamental. The relationship of these two tones (*C-G*) suggests the perfect fifth (see p. 154) as a basis of relationship between the tones of the major scale. (2) Parentheses have been placed around certain notes. This is done to indicate that, actually, the staff representations are not accurate indications of the true overtone pitches. This suggests that our system of tuning is a compromise between the natural harmonic relations and the need to make available twelve equal divisions within the octave.

The student may hear some of these upper partials or overtones by experimenting at the piano. For example, if he will raise the damper on small *c* by depressing the key, and strike and release great *C* (the octave below), the first overtone (the octave above) will be heard. In a similar manner, depress *G* and strike great *C*, and the second overtone (*G*) may be heard. In the same fashion, depress e^1, strike great *C*, and listen for the fourth overtone (e^1). It will be noted that the first overtone, the octave above great *C*, may be considered as a duplication of the fundamental. The second overtone is the twelfth, or *G* (which, for our purpose, may be reduced to the fifth).[1] This interval, the fifth, or any two tones which lie a perfect fifth apart, are in the closest possible harmonic relationship. With the next overtone we again discover the octave, again a duplication. The fourth overtone, e^1, however, stands in the relationship of a major third to the fundamental. These first several overtones, as can be easily seen, are the very familiar members of the tonic chord in the key of *C*.

As stated in the preceding paragraph, the closest possible relationship exists between tones standing a perfect fifth apart. The same is true of the relationship existing between scales, chords, and keys founded upon tones which lie a perfect fifth apart. To the introductory observations already made on the apparent kinship between scales with common tetrachords, a further one should be made concerning the tones of the principal chords of the major key, I, IV, and V: namely, that the chord members of these triads are derived from the overtones produced when their roots are used as the fundamental tone.

Ex. 9-5

Note in Ex. 9-5 that *C* is a perfect fifth above *F*, and *G* a perfect fifth above *C*. As stated immediately above, chords built upon these closely related tones stand in the same relationship as the tones themselves. Furthermore, the chord members derived from the overtones produced by *F*, *C*, and *G* as fundamentals are the tones of the scale and key of *C*.

Harmony

The subdominant chord in minor. The root of the subdominant chord in minor is found on the fourth tone of the scale, with its third and

[1] See Chapters 11 and 15 for information concerning intervals.

fifth on alternate degrees above. Shown below are its three positions in the key of *A* minor:

Ex. 9-6

(a) Position of the fifth, the fifth being highest

(b) Position of the root, the root being highest

(c) Position of the third, the third being highest

A fifth
F third
D root

D root
A fifth
F third

F third
D root
A fifth

IV

IV₆

IV⁶₄

(a) Fundamental position, the root being lowest

(b) First inversion, the third being lowest

(c) Second inversion, the fifth being lowest

The passing and neighboring tones are as follows:

Ex. 9-7

(a)

Passing Tones

(b)

Neighboring Tones

The conventional progressions of the I, IV, and V are shown below in the keys of A and C minor. Play them also in the keys of E and F minor, listening to the individual voices and the over-all effect.

Ex. 9-8

128

Observe how the I, IV, and V chords are employed in melody No. 5 from Melodies for Singing, especially the use of the second inversions of the tonic chord in the authentic cadence. Used in this manner, it is known as the cadential six-four.

Ex. 9-9

Use the following pattern in chording to Ex. 9-9.

Ex. 9-10

Melody No. 4 from Melodies for Singing is harmonized below for your study and analysis. Observe the distribution of voices, and the use of the $V\frac{6}{4}$. The latter as used here (passing from I to I_6 or vice versa) is known as the passing six-four.

Ex. 9-11

[2] Dominant seventh; see next chapter.

Swiss Folk Song

Rhythm

The dotted eighth and sixteenth in $\frac{6}{8}$ time.   Sing the following melody:

Ex. 9-12

This rhythm, the dotted eighth followed by the sixteenth in $\frac{6}{8}$ time, differs from that found in the preceding chapter (where the quarter note was used as the beat) in that, there the total time value of the two notes was one beat, whereas in the example above, the time value of the two notes is two beats. The result is triple groups in which unequal note values occur.

Melodies for Singing and Dictation

The following melodies contain examples of the melodic treatment of the tones of the subdominant chord in minor and the dotted-eighth-sixteenth rhythm in compound duple meter.

Melodies for Singing

3 Allegretto

mf I(f♯) Minor   IV   I   V   I   I

IV   I   V   I   I   I   V   I   V   I

I   I   V   I   V   I

MOUSSORGSKY

I $^6_4$ V♯   I

4 Allegro

mf I(a)   I6   V   I   V
    Minor

V   V   V   I $^6_4$ V   I   IV
Swiss Folk Song

V   I6   V $^6_4$ I   IV   I $^6_4$ V   I

5 Moderato

mf I(f) Minor I6   IV   I6(A♭) I Major   I6   I $^6_4$ Major V
Hebrew Melody

I(f) Minor V7   I   V   V6   I   I $^6_4$ V   I

6 Andante

f I   IV   I6   V7   I   I   IV

I6   V7   I

132

Russian Folk Song

IV   V₇   I

7 Andante

Russian Folk Song

8 Adagio

Russian Folk Song

9 Andantino

³ See page 170, Ex. 12-14 for explanation of the four-bar rest.

Home To Our Mountains   From Il Trovatore   VERDI

10   Allegro

Old French Song

11   Poco Animato

Spring Dreams   SCHUBERT

12   Allegro Moderato

[4] The small note is known as an acciaccatura and should be sung as quickly as possible with the accent upon the principal note.

Melodies for Dictation

Suggestions for Further Study

Write the attendant scales of the keys of G, D, A, F, Bb, and Eb, at (a) in the Work Sheet.

Write the subdominant chord in the major keys. Convert each to a minor triad by lowering the third.

Work Sheet

D

A

F

B♭

E♭

10

Dynamics

Rudiments

Degrees of sound-volume. Of great importance to the expressive performance of music is its relative loudness and softness, or *dynamics*. The ability to recognize dynamic markings and to interpret them in terms of effective performance is as important as the ability to hear tones. By means of special words, abbreviations, and signs the composer is able to indicate the degree of dynamics he desires. A brief list of these follow:

Piano   *p* —softly
Forte   *f* —loudly
Forzando *fz*
Sforzando *sf, sfz*
Forzato *fz*
Sforzato *sf, sfz*
    or > ∧

These words and signs indicate that a tone or a chord is to receive special stress or accent.

Crescendo (cres. or ═══ —gradually louder
Decrescendo (decresc. or ══ —gradually softer
Diminuendo (dim. or ═══ —gradually softer
Amore—tenderness, affection
Bravura—boldness, spirit
Energia—energy, force
Espressione—expression, feeling
Brio—vigor, animation
Fuoco—fire, energy
Passione—passion, feeling
Grazia—grace, elegance
Tenerezza—tenderness, delicacy

Dolce—sweetly, softly
Maestoso—majestic, stately
Pomposo—pompously
Sotto Voce—subdued voice

These terms may be combined with others found in Chapter 6 dealing with tempo.

The double period.   The *double period,* when regular, consists of four phrases, representing a combination of two single periods. In the same fashion that the antecedent and consequent phrases of an individual period depend on each other, the two periods of a double period are mutually dependent. The first phrase of the double period usually ends on the third or fifth tone of the scale (tonic chord), whereas the second phrase closes with a half cadence (dominant chord). The third phrase may end in a manner similar to that of the first phrase, but it often moves toward the subdominant chord. The fourth phrase, as may be expected, closes with the perfect authentic cadence. Examples of melodies in this form are as follows: p. 66, No. 3; p. 83, No. 10; p. 174, No. 1.

Harmony

The dominant seventh in minor.   The *dominant seventh in minor* is built on the fifth tone of the scale. It, like any chord of the seventh, consists of four tones on alternate staff degrees. Since the three upper tones of the chord are active, they demand, when sounded together, a resolution to rest tones. The chord in its four positions is shown in Ex. 10-1.

Ex. 10-1

(a) Position of the 7th,
the 7th being highest

(a) Fundamental position,
the root being lowest

(b) Position of the root,
the root being highest

(b) First inversion,
the 3rd being lowest

(c) Position of the 3rd,
the 3rd being highest

(c) Second inversion,
the 5th being lowest

(d) Position of the 5th,
the 5th being highest

(d) Third inversion,
the 7th being lowest

The passing and neighboring tones (other than those given for the dominant, Chapter 8) are as follows:

Ex. 10-2

The conventional progressions of the I, IV, V₇, and I are shown in Ex. 10-3 in the keys of A and D minor. Play them also in the keys of B and G minor, observing the voice leadings, and listening to individual voices as well as the total effect.

Ex. 10-3

Observe the use of the I and V₇ chords in melody No. 1 from Melodies for Singing.

Ex. 10-4

Use the following pattern in chording to Ex. 10-4:

Ex. 10-5

Note the distributing of voices in the harmonization of this melody.

Ex. 10-6

Rhythm

The triplet. Sing the following well known melody:

Ex. 10–7

Notice the groups of three notes joined together by a curved line and designated by the figure three. These are known as *triplets* and are executed in the time of two tones of like value. In "Juanita" the three eighth-note groups are sung in the time equivalent of two eighth notes. The first note of the group is accented.

Triplets may be formed of notes of any length, or of a combination of notes and rests, as in the following:

Ex. 10–8

Melodies for Singing and Dictation

The following melodies contain examples of the dominant seventh chord in minor and triplets.

Melodies for Singing

2 Allegro Con Brio

I(f) Minor   I   V7   I

I   I   V7   I

Refrain, Audacious Tar   From H. M. S. Pinafore   SULLIVAN

3 Moderato

I(g) Minor   V7   I   V

I   V7   I   V7   I   I   V

Norwegian Folk Song

V   I   IV   I   V7   I

4 Un Poco Piu Lento

I (ab) Minor   V7   I

I   V7

Can I Survive This Overbearing   From H. M. S. Pinafore   SULLIVAN

I⁶₄   V7   I

5 Andante

145

Death of Ase   From Peer Gynt Suite   GRIEG

6   Allegro
I(d) Minor   V   I   I   V   I   I(F) Major (F)
V

Things Are Seldom What They Seem   From H. M. S. Pinafore   SULLIVAN
I(F)   V(F)   I(d) Minor   V   I   V₇   I

7   Adagio

To The Waiter   SCHUMANN

8   Allegro
I(e) Minor   V₇   I   V₇
I(G) Major   V₇(G)

Molly's Hoop   Old English Melody
I(G)   V₇(G)   I(e) V₇   V   V₇   I

9   Allegro
I(g)   V   I   V   I   I   V(B♭) Major
I(B♭)   I(B♭)   V(B♭)   V₇

146

Three Merry Men of Kent   English Melody

Pilgrim's Chorus   From Tannhäuser   WAGNER

Serenade   SCHUBERT

The Linden Tree   SCHUBERT

13   Moderato

14   Allegretto Con Brio

Woman's Unfeeling Heart   From Rigoletto   VERDI

15   Andante

Funeral March   MENDELSSOHN

148

Melodies for Dictation

Suggestions for Further Study

Write the dominant seventh chord in the minor keys (see Chapter 8, p. 110 concerning the raised third).

Examine several of your favorite compositions for examples of the triplet and dynamics.

Work Sheet

11

Major, Perfect and Minor Intervals

Rudiments

Classification of intervals. The difference in pitch between two tones, as we have already learned, is called an interval. In Ex. 11-1 below are two intervals that the student should play on the piano:

Ex. 11-1

Two observations may be made with regard to this example which will help us to understand more clearly the nature of intervals. (1) Although there is a similarity between these intervals in that each involves three degrees of the staff—C, D, E—they actually sound different when played on the piano. (2) The difference in the sounds of these intervals results from the fact that they are different in size; that is, each contains a different number of half steps: the first one, C to E, four half steps; the second, C to E♭, three half steps. On the basis of these observations it may be stated that intervals are classified in two ways: according to the number of staff degrees involved and according to the number of half steps contained. The first gives us the general name of the interval and the second the particular name. The intervals in Ex. 11-1 are thirds, embracing as they do three degrees of the staff—C, D, and E. This is their general name. Their particular name is determined by counting the number of half steps contained. However, a more convenient method for arriving at their particular name is normally used, the basis of which is the application of the major scale. For example, an interval from the key tone of the major scale to any other tone of the major scale is either *major* or *perfect*. Examine the following:

Ex. 11-2

Major and perfect intervals. Note that the interval from 1 to 2 of any major scale is a major second; from 1 to 3, a major third; from 1 to 6, a major sixth; from 1 to 7, a major seventh; from 1 to 9, a major ninth; and similarly that the interval from 1 to 1 is a perfect prime; from 1 to 4, a perfect fourth; from 1 to 5, a perfect fifth; and from 1 to 8, a perfect octave.[2] *Note:* this should be committed to memory, for it will be used as the basis for calculating all other intervals.

It may be stated as a general rule that the particular name of any interval is determined by its relation to the major scale, by whether the upper tone of the interval occurs as a tone of the major scale, or whether the upper tone of the interval is higher or lower than the corresponding tone of the major scale.

Minor intervals. The minor intervals have the same general name as the major—that is, they have the same number of degrees of the staff—but since they are one half step smaller, the upper tone of the interval being lower than the corresponding tone in the major scale, the particular name is different. The minor intervals with their particular names are illustrated in the following:[3]

Ex. 11-3

Melodic and harmonic intervals; major and minor chords. An interval is melodic when the two tones are heard in succession. Examine the following example:

Ex. 11-4

These are, of course, thirds, even though they are not sounded simultaneously. Now using our general rule we can also determine their particular names. Considering *E* as the key tone of the *E*-major scale, then *G♯* in *A* in Ex. 11-4 is the third tone of the *E*-major scale, and therefore a major third. In *B*, consider *E* again as the key tone of the *E*-major scale. In this case, however, *G* is smaller by one half step than the third tone of the *E*-major scale, and the interval is, therefore, a minor third.

An interval is harmonic when the tones are heard simultaneously. Since this phenomenon is quite common in chords, let us examine the harmonic intervals of chords we have studied in the past, for instance, the I, IV, V, and V_7 in the major and minor keys.

Ex. 11-5

In the Tonic, the interval of *C* to *E* is a major third, that from *C* to *G*, a perfect fifth. The subdominant IV and the dominant V also have a major third and a perfect fifth: namely, *F* to *A* and *F* to *C* in the subdominant, and *G* to *B* and *G* to *D* in the dominant. Thus each chord contains the intervals of a major third and a perfect fifth. On the basis of the thirds contained, the lower third of the chords is a major third and the upper third a minor third. Any triad with these intervals is called a *major chord*.

Now let us consider the intervals of these chords as they occur in *C*-minor:

Ex. 11-6

To summarize:

Tonic: C to E♭, minor third; C to G, perfect fifth
Subdominant: F to A♭, minor third: F to C, perfect fifth
Dominant: G to B, major third; G to D, perfect fifth

Thus the I and IV chords contain the intervals of a minor third, and a perfect fifth. Considering the thirds, the lower third of the chord is minor, the upper third, major. Any triad with these intervals is a *minor chord.* The V chord, in *C* above, has a major third rather than a minor third, though it does have the perfect fifth. The V chord, in other words, is the same as it is in the major key.

The dominant seventh, like the dominant, is invariable; that is, its intervals are the same in both the major and minor key. The dominant seventh is shown below in *C*-major and *C*-minor:

Ex. 11-7

G to B, is a major third; G to D, a perfect fifth; G to F, a minor seventh.

Harmony

Review of harmony. In the preceding chapters we have studied the principal triads (I, IV, and V) in both the major and minor key, as well as the dominant seventh chord in the major and minor key. We may now briefly review these chords and their interval content:

1. A triad is formed by adding a third and fifth to a given tone called the root.
2. Any member of the chord may occur as the highest tone of the chord.
3. Any member of the chord may occur as the lowest tone of the chord.
4. If the third of a triad is major and the fifth is perfect, the chord is major. The tonic, dominant, and subdominant triads in the major key are major chords.
5. If the third of a triad is minor and the fifth is perfect, the chord is minor. The tonic and subdominant chords in the minor key are minor; the dominant, on the other hand, is major.
6. By adding a third to the dominant triad we get the tones of the dominant seventh chord. The intervals of this chord in both the major and minor key are a major third, a perfect fifth, and a minor seventh.

Melody No. 11 from Melodies for Singing, Chapter 10, is harmonized below for observation and study. This example illustrates the contrasts between the major and minor harmonies discussed in this chapter. Note especially the change from one key to another, and that a V_7 chord in the new key initiates the change.

Ex. 11-8

4 Here the composer has skipped to a non-harmonic tone. This is called an appoggiatura.

Rhythm

Compound triple meter.   When there are nine units of rhythm in a measure, they fall into three groups of three units each, forming a *compound triple* meter having the effect of a simple triple meter such as $\frac{3}{4}$ employing triplets. The accents fall on the first of each triple group, or on beats one, four, and seven. If the tempo is rapid, there will be only three beats in each measure because each group of three beats is felt as one beat. This is usually known as compound triple meter. An interesting experiment may be made by writing a measure of "Juanita," first in its proper $\frac{3}{4}$ meter, then in $\frac{9}{8}$ time, thus:

Ex. 11–9

NI - TA   JUA - - NI - TA

Ex. 11–10

ni - ta   Jua - - ni - ta

In the first representation, each quarter note or its equivalent gets a beat; in the second, the dotted quarter note or equivalent. Actually, to the ear they are the same.

Melodies for Singing and Dictation

As may have been observed, no new chord was introduced in this chapter. Instead the stress was on intervals as they occur between the successive tones in melody and as they occur in chords. In the melodies which follow, the student will find intervals of a wide variety which he has not encountered heretofore. These should be given special attention. The melodies also contain examples in compound triple meter.

Melodies for Singing

Lithuanian Folk Song

4 Andante

From Symphony No. 94   HAYDN

5 Largo

Behold, And See If There Be Any Sorrow   From The Messiah   HANDEL

6 Andante

Thou Shalt Break Them   From The Messiah   HANDEL

7 Allegretto

With Joy Th' Impatient Husbandman   From The Seasons   HAYDN

8 Adagio

O God, Have Mercy   From St. Paul   MENDELSSOHN

9 Largo

I (A)   I (C)   I   V₇

I   IV   I   V₇

Over The Bright Blue Sea   From H. M. S. Pinafore   SULLIVAN

I   V₇   I

14   Grazioso   The Message   BRAHMS

p

15   Lento

p

Not a Breath in Heaven Stirs   BRAHMS

16   Lento   Lamentation MOUSSORGSKY

mp

17   Andante   Have You Heard of a Frolicsome Ditty?   PEPUSCH

mf

Melodies for Dictation

1   Allegro   He More Knightly Than The Noblest   SCHUMANN

p

13 Allegro Assai Vivace   Spring Song   MENDELSSOHN

14 Andante   Song of the Rhinemaidens   WAGNER

15 Andante   In This Hour of the Night   TSCHAIKOWSKY

16 Andante   Speak Not, O Beloved   TSCHAIKOWSKY

17 Andante   Sorry Her Lot   From H. M. S. Pinafore   SULLIVAN

Suggestions for Further Study

Identify the intervals on the work sheet, giving both the general and the specific names. Play each tone of the interval in succession and then simultaneously, listening to the effect.

Write the I, IV, V and V_7 chords in the keys of G major and G minor. Indicate the intervals of each chord. Play them, listening to the total effect.

Identify the melodic intervals in melodies 1, 3, and 4 in Melodies for Singing.

Work Sheet

G Major   G Minor

I   IV   V   V₇   I   IV   V   V₇

12

Additional Symbols Used in Music

Rudiments

Miscellaneous signs. The *fermata* is the Italian term for the sign ⌒ , in English usually called a *hold*. It signifies that the note or rest over which it is placed is to be prolonged beyond its natural duration. There is no rule concerning the length of the increased duration, this being left to the judgment of the performer. The fermata is also placed over a measure bar or a double bar to indicate a short period of silence.

The slur, introduced in an earlier chapter relative to its use in singing, is also used extensively in instrumental music to indicate a special phrasing effect. When it is placed over or under a group of notes, they are to be performed with the smoothness more commonly expressed by the term *legato*. Play the following examples, observing the use of this important phrasing device.

Ex. 12-1

Waltz No. 15   BRAHMS

Ex. 12-2

Dots over or under the notes indicate an effect just the opposite of that indicated by the slur or phrase mark—indicating, rather, that the tones are to be detached. *Note:*

Ex. 12-3

Ex. 12-4

Tones so indicated are to be made shorter and to be separated by periods of silence, as though they were played or sung as follows:

Ex. 12-5

Sometimes the slur and the *staccato,* are combined:

Ex. 12-6

The tones are to be detached, but with briefer periods of silence, thus:

Ex. 12-7

This is known as *mezzo staccato,* or *portato.*

The *arpeggio sign* ⦃, placed before a chord, suggests that the tones, beginning with the lowest, are to be played as a rapid succession of tones. The result is a harp-like effect.

Ex. 12-8

The octave transposition sign, *8va,* followed by a dotted line, signifies that the notes are to be played an octave higher than written. The notes so affected are those embraced by the sign itself and the line, thus:

Ex. 12-9

Where the composer wishes the notes to be played an octave lower, in the bass, he uses the signs *8va bassa* or *8va sotta.* If the note is to be accompanied by its octave either above or below, the terms *Con 8va* or *All 8va* are placed above or below the note:

Ex. 12-10

In orchestral music, one or more lines drawn through a stem of a note indicate that the note is to be repeated: a single line indicates the repetition is to be eighth notes, a double line, sixteenths.

Ex. 12-11

The same shorthand device is also used for notes on different degrees of the staff.

Ex. 12-12

A sign for the repetition of a group of notes in orchestral music is ⅞. Its use is illustrated in the following:

Ex. 12-13

Silent measures in any musical score are indicated by the whole rest sign with a number placed above to indicate the number of measures to be silent.

Ex. 12-14

A number of methods are used where sections of music are to be repeated. The sign for the repetition of a whole section of a composition is a double perpendicular bar and a row of dots. For example:

Ex. 12-15

Repeat from the beginning of the composition

Repeat the section between the double bars and dots

If the repeated portion is to end differently from the first, it is indicated in the following manner:

Ex. 12-16

Sometimes the term *Da Capo* (from the beginning, abbreviated *D.C.*) placed at the end of a section is used to indicate a repeat from the beginning. The term *D. C. al Fine* is also used. In this case, the repeated portion ends with the bar over which the word *Fine* again appears. The term *Dal Segno* (from the sign, abbreviated *D.S.*) appearing at the end of a section directs the performer to repeat, beginning from a point marked by the sign: ✗. The word *Fine* again marks the end of the repetition. The *coda* sign ⊕ used at some point in a repeated portion, indicates that a skip is to be made from that point to the coda or closing portion of the composition.

The use of the damper pedal on the piano is indicated by the abbreviation *Ped.*, and its use terminates with the appearance of the sign *. The following signs are also used:

Ex. 12-17

The supertonic chord. We have learned that the principal chords of the major key are the tonic (I), the dominant (V), and the subdominant (IV). The major key also has chords called *secondary chords,* the names of which are the *supertonic* (II), the *mediant* (III), and the *submediant* (VI). All of these secondary triads are minor chords.

The most important of these triads is the supertonic (above tonic), formed on the second degree of the scale. It is used in fundamental position and in the first inversion, but rarely in the second inversion. It is shown below in the two positions in which it is most frequently found.

Ex. 12-18

Its intervals are a minor third and a perfect fifth. The passing and neighboring tones are the same as for the IV in the minor key (except for the chromatically raised seventh of the minor scale), which may be found in Chapter 9, p. 128.

Conventional progressions involving the supertonic chord are shown below in the keys of C and A flat. In addition to these keys, play the examples in F and G, listening to the individual voices and the total effect.

Ex. 12-19

Observe the use of the two-six chord in melody No. 10 from Melodies for Singing. Can you fake a bass to this melody as well as melodies 1, 3, and 13?

Ex. 12-20

I   I6   II6   V   V

Give Me Your Hand Zerlina   MOZART

I   I6   II6   V   V7   I

Rhythm

Compound quadruple meter. When there are 12 units of rhythm in a measure, they fall into four groups of three units each, forming a compound quadruple meter having the effect of a simple quadruple meter such as $\frac{4}{4}$ employing triplets. The accents fall on the first of each triple group, or on beats one, four, seven, and ten. If the tempo is rapid, the conductor's pattern calls for only four beats in each measure. This is usually known as *compound quadruple meter.*

Melody No. 20 in Melodies for Singing includes rhythmic problems of considerable complexity for the beginner. The first approach to feeling this rhythm is through counting twelve beats to the measure, each eighth note receiving one beat. With this approach, the sixteenth notes become equal divisions and the thirty-second notes equal subdivisions of the beat. The student should be cautioned to maintain a legato singing style. When these divisions are understood and felt, four beats to the measure should be used with particular attention being given to the note on which each beat occurs.

Melodies for Singing and Dictation

The following melodies contain examples of the supertonic chord and of compound quadruple meter.

Melodies for Singing

Oh, Praise The Lord   From Athalie   MENDELSSOHN

II   V   I   IV   I$^6_4$ V   I

5   Allegro

Intermezzo, Op. 61, No. 5   MENDELSSOHN

6   Allegretto

I   I   I   I   II

II   II   I   I

Love Is Like a Wild Bird Rebelling   From Carmen   BIZET

I   II   II   II   V$_7$ I

7   Allegro Moderato

I   I   V$^6_5$ V$^6_5$

17 Allegro Moderato

Torments of Hate and Vengeance From Lucia di Lammermoor DONIZETTI

18 Andante Moto

Charity ROSSINI

19 Largo

I Think of Thee SCHUBERT

20 Larghetto

Pastoral Symphony From Messiah HANDEL

Melodies for Dictation

1 Allegro

German Folk Song

Suggestions for Further Study

Examine several of your favorite compositions for examples of the symbols presented in this chapter.

Examine an orchestral score for examples of symbols for repeated passages.

Identify the intervals on the work sheet. Play each tone of the interval, first successively, then simultaneously, listening to the effect.

Write the I, IV, V and V_7 chords in the keys of *F* major and *F* minor. Indicate the intervals of each chord. Play them, listening to the total effect.

Work Sheet

13

Elementary
Musical Forms

Rudiments

A review of form. In each of the preceding chapters we have been dealing with, and giving emphasis to, the elements of *form*. Our first experience was with the orderly grouping of the strong and weak *accents* into measures. Later we observed that measures were grouped into phrases, and phrases into periods. Again, it was discovered that even the arrangement of rhythmic patterns within the phrase was evidence of order. The second major experience had to do with the grouping of *tones* into phrases. We observed that the antecedent and consequent phrases were united into a period by parallel and contrasting construction, and that two periods, when combined, formed the double period. Even the melodic movement, with its relationship to the chord, was thus suggestive of design. The third experience was with *harmony*. The chord changes usually occurred upon the accented part of the measure, and the particular type of cadence was determined by the use of a certain chord, or chords. Even the folk and art melodies within the preceding chapters suggest harmonic schemes.

Thus the three elements of music—rhythm, melody, and harmony—constitute the very essence of form, being elements so interdependent and so inseparably bound that it is difficult to think of one without the other. The folk and composed melodies, in their rhythmic and harmonic settings, bear witness of the symmetry, design, balance, and beauty of form.

Plagal and deceptive cadences. From our earlier study of cadence, it will be recalled that the half-cadence consisted of dominant harmonies at the close of a phrase; that the dominant to tonic progression, with the root of the chord in the melody, resulted in the perfect authentic cadence; and that the same harmonies (dominant to tonic) with the third or fifth of the chord in the melody brought about the imperfect authentic cadence.

There remain now but two new cadences for our consideration. The first of these consists of a subdominant to tonic progression, as found in the familiar church *amen:*

Ex. 13–1

This is known as the *plagal cadence* and is often added as an extension of the phrase ending with the perfect authentic cadence. This is easily discernible in many hymns.

The second cadence to be considered is the *deceptive* or *interrupted* close. This occurs when the dominant or dominant seventh resolves to any unexpected chord. A good example is found in the Handel Largo, where the dominant harmonies progress to the submediant (VI),[1] as shown below:

Ex. 13–2

Other form elements. With this background, we are now ready to make further observations concerning form. First let us sing an interesting phrase from Verdi's *Il Trovatore:*

[1] See p. 187.

Ex. 13-3

Now contrast it with the following familiar melody from Mozart's The Marriage of Figaro:

Ex. 13-4

It is quite evident that the composers of these two melodies have taken a group of three tones in a simple rhythmic pattern and repeated them, either at the same pitch or by sequence. This small group of tones, as we have already learned, is called a *figure* and is the smallest of musical ideas. The student will also find "When Love Is Kind," p. 177, No. 13, interesting from this standpoint.

Now sing this familiar melody from Dvorak's Symphony No. 5.

Ex. 13-5

Here again the composer has used a small group of tones, extending them into a well-balanced melody. Note that the repetitions are more varied than in Exs. 13-3 and 13-4. Note also that in measures 5, 6, 7, and 8, the composer has changed the direction of the third and altered the rhythm to give variety. We may conclude from these observations that *repetition— exact or in sequence—is one of the fundamental principles of form,* and that a phrase or even a longer passage is often developed from a very small group of tones.

Binary form. Sing the following melody:

Ex. 13-6

French Folk Song

This folk song consists of two different melodic parts, each of which ends with the perfect cadence. But, though the two parts are different, they seem to belong together. Such combinations of parts unlike in melody, where the second part acts as a response to the first, are known as *binary* or *two-part* form, often designated as A-B form. Other examples are melodies No. 3, p. 159; No. 8, p. 82; and No. 1, p. 113.

Ternary form.   Sing the following melody—"Old Folks at Home" by Stephen C. Foster.

Ex. 13-7

Analyzing this melody, we find the following features:

1. The first phrase ends on the dominant chord to form the half-cadence.
2. The second phrase ends on the tonic preceded by the dominant to form the authentic cadence.
3. The first two phrases are identical except at the cadence.
4. The tone at the cadence (the dotted half) is longer than the preceding tones.
5. The cadence in each case falls on the strong part of the measure.
6. The third phrase is unlike the others.
7. The fourth phrase condenses the original thought by repeating only phrase two.
8. In this melody, A is a parallel period, and B and A are phrases.

From these observations it may be concluded that all phrases end with a cadence, that the cadence is often made more prominent by a long tone, and that it occurs on the accented part of the measure. Observations 6 and 7 suggest the basis of *ternary* or *three-part form,* often designated as *A-B-A.* According to Observation 6, the third phrase in Ex. 13-7 is a distinct digression from the original idea; according to Observation 7, the fourth phrase is a restatement or recapitulation of the original thought. The ternary form may be defined, then, as a statement, digression, and restatement of musical ideas. The length of each part in a simple ternary form may vary, but the basic design remains stable. Other examples of the *A-B-A* form are melodies No. 12, p. 53, No. 2, p. 114 and No. 3, p. 114.

Note: Although the ideas expressed in this chapter and its examples concern only the smallest of musical forms, they reveal the basic principles upon which the larger forms of music are also based.

Harmony

The submediant chord. The *submediant chord* is that secondary triad next in importance to the supertonic. Since its tones and intervals are the same as those of the tonic chord in the minor key, the student will encounter no difficulty in singing the melodies in this chapter. It is built on the sixth tone of the scale and often follows the dominant or the dominant seventh instead of the tonic. It is also used as a connecting link between the tonic and subdominant chords. Since the passing and neighboring tones of this chord are the same as for the tonic triad in the minor key (except for the chromatically raised seventh tone of the minor scale), the student is referred to them, Chapter 7, p. 94. The submediant chord is shown below in fundamental position and first inversion, the ways it is most frequently found.

Ex. 13-8

Conventional progressions involving the submediant chord are shown below in the keys of C and E. Play them also in the keys of D and B flat. At (a) the dominant seventh resolves to the submediant instead of the tonic thus affecting a deceptive cadence. Observe also the use of the cadential six-four at (b) and (c).

Ex. 13-9

Melody No. 1 from Melodies for Singing is harmonized below for study and observation. Note the use of the submediant chord.

Ex. 13-10

The Lord's My Shepherd HAVERGAL

Can you fake a bass to melody No. 4?

Rhythm

Syncopation. *Syncopation* is a rhythmic phenomenon which results when the normal expected pulsation of meter, accent, and rhythm pattern is upset. As we have already learned, rhythm is based upon the combining of the beats into groups of two and three, having a regular recurring accent on the first beat of each group. The upsetting of the normal rhythm, which we call syncopation, is accomplished by shifting the stress to the normally weak accents. Note the following examples. At (a) the normal pulsation is upset by the tie which forces the accent to fall on the weak

Ex. 13-11

part of the measure. At (b) syncopation is brought about in two ways: first, by the quarter notes on E and C falling on the unaccented part of the beat, and second, by holding the eighth note over the measure bar into the strong accent. At (c) the regular pulsation of the meter is upset by the rests which occur on the strong part of measures 2, 4, and 6.

Syncopation also results from accenting an unaccented part of the measure, as Beethoven did in the Scherzo of the Eroica Symphony.

Ex. 13-12

The student will find interesting examples of syncopation in Chapter 12, melody No. 17, p. 178, and melody No. 20, p. 178.

Melodies for Singing and Dictation

The following melodies contain examples of the chord tones of the submediant, and of syncopation.

Melodies for Singing

3 Andante Moderato

mp

Lord, Make Me to Know   From Requiem   BRAHMS

4 Vivace

f I   I   V V₆   V V₆   I

IV II   V   V₆V₇ I V I   I   V₇   VI

English Folk Song

V   I   IV   II   V   V₆ V₇   I V₇ I

5 Allegretto

mp

Morning   From Peer Gynt Suite   GRIEG

6 Allegro

f

II

III

Round   PURCELL

7   Andante   From Symphony No. 6   TSCHAIKOWSKY

8   Tempo di Marcia

American Army Song

9   Moderato , Ma Animato

Lo, How a Rose   PRAETORIOUS

10   Allegro Moderato

Czechoslovakian Folk Song

192

11 Andante Molto

mf

Moonlight and Roses LEMARE

12 Andante

p

rit.

Highland Cradle Song SCHUMANN

13 Allegro Hallelujah From Messiah HANDEL

ff I IV I I IV I IV I I IV I V I

14 Larghetto

f

Blessing and Honor From Messiah HANDEL

15 Allegro

mf

² There is a modulation to F sharp minor in the sixth measure of this melody.

Sanctus, Requiem   VERDI

16   Andante

Ev'ry Valley Shall Be Exalted   From Messiah   HANDEL

17   Allegro Molto   From Symphony No. 5   DVORAK

Melodies for Dictation

1   Moderato   Now Let Every Tongue Adore Thee   BACH

2   Vivace   English Folk Song

3   Andante   Farewell to the Forest   MENDELSSOHN

4   Moderato   Irish

5 Piu Adagio   Cast Thy Burden Upon The Lord   From Elijah   MENDELSSOHN

6 Andante   Spanish Folk Song

7 Allegretto   I'm Called Little Buttercup From H. M. S. Pinafore   SULLIVAN

8 Allegro   From Symphony No. 5   DVORAK

9 Tempo di Marcia   American Army Song

10 Allegro Moderato   Czechoslovakian Folk Song

11 Moderato   Negro Spiritual

12 Tempo di Valse   Love Songs   Waltz No. 13   BRAHMS

13 Andante   Scotch Folk Song

14 Moderato   Scotch Folk Song

15 Lively   Lieder No. 1   SCHUMANN

195

Suggestions for Further Study

Examine several of your favorite compositions for examples of the various cadences.

Listen for examples of repetition, exact or in sequence, in your favorite recordings.

Find examples of syncopation in a Bach, Beethoven, and Schumann composition.

Identify the intervals on the work sheet. Play the lower tone; sing the upper; test by playing each in succession. Play the lower tone again. Can you imagine the total effect if both tones were sounded simultaneously? Try it, and then test by playing.

Work Sheet

14

The Chromatic Scale

Rudiments

Construction of the chromatic scale.   Begin at Middle *C* and play successively all the white and black keys through an octave. This series of tones is known as the *chromatic* scale (Greek: *chroma*, color). It is built entirely upon half steps, the octave being divided into twelve equal parts. The new tones added between *C* and *D*, *D* and *E*, *F* and *G*, *G* and *A*, and *A* and *B* are called chromatic tones, and are foreign to the key—that is, they are not diatonic tones. Obviously these alien tones are possible only at points where there is an interval of a whole step (a major second). In the major scale there are five such intervals, and therefore five new tones may be added. These, of course, are represented on the staff by sharps, flats, naturals, double sharps, and double flats.

Of the several possible ways of writing this series of tones known as the chromatic scale, the simplest is the notation employed in the melodic form shown below in the key of *C*, *D♭*, and *E* major.

Ex. 14–1

In the ascending scales above, it will be noted that each new chromatic tone is derived from the *lower* diatonic tone immediately preceding, which has been raised. In the descending scale the new tones are derived from the preceding *upper* diatonic tone. The one exception here is that the raised fourth is used instead of the lowered fifth. The names of the chromatic tones are likewise derived from the diatonic tones; for example, C, C♯, D, D♯, for the ascending, and C, B, B♭, A, A♭, for the descending. To secure the new syllabic names for the raised tones, the original vowels are changed to "i" (pronounced "ee"). For the lowered tones, the vowel is changed to "e" (pronounced "ay"). One exception in this respect is *re*, which already has the vowel "e." When re is lowered, the spelling is changed to *ra* and it is pronounced "rah."

The spelling of the chromatic scale in minor differs from major as shown below in the key of *C* minor:

Ex. 14-2

Augmented and diminished intervals. In Chapter 11 we learned that an interval from the key tone of the major scale to any other tone of the scale is either major or perfect. The major intervals, we learned, are the second, third, sixth, seventh, and ninth; the perfect intervals, the prime, fourth, fifth, and octave. The minor intervals—the minor second, third, sixth, seventh, and ninth—are the same as the major except that each is a half step smaller than the corresponding major. These are shown below for review.

Ex. 14-3

In addition to the three classes of intervals just mentioned, there are two others, the *augmented* and the *diminished*. The augmented intervals have the same general name as the *major* and *perfect,* but are one half step *larger*. The diminished intervals have the same general name as the *minor* and *perfect,* but are one half step *smaller*. These are illustrated below:

Ex. 14-4

Intervals may be further classified as consonant and dissonant. The dissonant intervals, because of their active nature, are normally resolved to the consonant. Examining the intervals already discussed on the basis of consonance and dissonance, it may be pointed out that the perfect intervals are called perfect consonants; major and minor thirds and sixths, imperfect consonants; major and minor seconds and sevenths, and all augmented and diminished intervals, dissonances.

An interval may be inverted by taking the lower tone and placing it an octave higher, or by placing the upper tone an octave lower, as shown in Ex. 14-5.

[1] These intervals are rare in music because they contain the same number of half steps as a perfect interval. Doubly augmented and diminished intervals also occur in music but quite rarely.

Ex. 14-5

It will be noted that when it is inverted the perfect interval remains perfect—hence its name; the major becomes minor; the minor becomes major; the augmented becomes diminished; and the diminished becomes augmented. It should also be noted that the general name is changed in every case: the fifth becomes a fourth, the fourth becomes a fifth, and so on.

Harmony

The mediant chord. The *mediant chord,* built on the third tone of the scale, is the least important of the secondary triads. It, like the other secondary chords, is minor, having a minor third and a perfect fifth. Its principal use is to harmonize the seventh degree of the scale in a descending passage. It is shown below in fundamental position and first inversion, as it is most frequently found.

Ex. 14-6

Conventional progressions involving the mediant and the supertonic sixth are shown below in the keys of C and B flat. Play them also in the keys of B and D flat. Observe the contrary motion from the mediant to the subdominant between which chords there is no common tone.

Ex. 14-7

I III IV II6 I⁶₄ V7 I   I III IV II6 I⁶₄ V7 I

Observe in *Old Hundredth* the use of all chords we have studied.

Ex. 14-8

I   V VI III VI V I   V7 VI   IV I V VI

Old Hundreth   Bourgeois

V I V I6 IV V I   VI V II   I6 V~7 I

Rhythm

Review of rhythm. In the preceding chapters we have studied the typical rhythms as found in the six meters most frequently used in music. These included the various relative note and rest lengths, the divided beat and sub-divided beat, the dotted half, quarter, and eighth, the tie, and the triplet. The melodies found in the accompanying Melodies for Singing illustrate these rhythms and will serve as a review.

Melodies for Singing and Dictation

The following melodies contain a review of the rhythms studied in previous chapters, chromatic tones, and the chord tones of the mediant triad.

Melodies for Singing

1 Presto

Rondo Trio No. 1   HAYDN

2 Andantino

I Dreamt That I Dwelt in Marble Halls   From Bohemian Girl   BALFE

3 Adagio

Sweet Genevieve   TUCKER

4 Andantino
Dolce

Song of India   RIMSKY-KORSAKOV

2 See footnote on page 127.

5 Allegro

Shadow Song   From Dinorah   MEYERBEER

6 Adagio

Ah Must Ye Fade   From La Sonnambula   BELLINI

7 Largo

Praise of Tears   SCHUBERT

8 Lento Expressione

Elegie MASSENET

9 Allegro Moderato

Toreador Song From Carmen BIZET

10 Lento

The Lotus-Flower SCHUMANN

11 Andante con Moto

From Symphony No. 5 BEETHOVEN

12 Andante

p *pp* *f*

p

I Love Thee   GRIEG

f *ff*

13 Andantino

p

Goodbye   TOSTI

14 Andante con Moto

f I   IV   II   V   III   VI

IV   V   I   III   IV   V

English Folk Song

I   I   IV   V   I

15 Andante con Moto
Tenerezza

p

Songs My Mother Taught Me   DVORAK

206

16 Andantino

p I VI I VI I VI III

Obstination   FONTENAILLES

II V₇ I III V₇ I

17 Semlice

p I V I V₇ IV I VI

The Swallow's Song   RADECKE

III VI I V₇ I

18 Moderato Maestoso

ff I I II I VI

I III III V

II II

Redeemed   From Faust   GOUNOD

III III VI I V I

19 Allegro

f I I6 V⁴₃ V III VI V I I6

Glory to Egypt   From Aida   VERDI

IV I (Minor) I6 II I6 IV I⁶₄ V₇ I

207

Melodies for Dictation

1 Adagio   Sweet Genevive   TUCKER

2 Andantino   I Dreamt That I Dwelt in Marble Halls   From Bohemian Girl   BALFE

3 Adagio   Ah, Must Ye Fade   From La Sonnambula   BELLINI

4 Semplice   The Swallow's Song   RADECKE

5 Andante con Moto   English Folk Song

6 Allegretto, Quasi Andantino   Habanera   From Carmen   BIZET

7 Andante   Evening Star   From Tannhäuser   WAGNER

8 Andatino   Goodbye   TOSTI

Suggestions for Further Study

Write the chromatic scale ascending and descending on the work sheet at (a), in the keys of *F, Eb, Gb, G, D, B* and *F♯* major.

Write the I, II, III, IV, V, V₇ and VI chords in the keys of *Eb,* and *A* major on the work sheet at (b). Indicate the intervals in each chord and show whether it is major or minor. Play the chords, listening to the total effect.

Identify the intervals at (c) on the work sheet.

Invert the intervals at (d) on the work sheet and identify.

Identify the successive intervals in melody No. 4 in Melodies for Singing above.

Work Sheet

15

Coda

During the preceding fourteen chapters, our study has covered the following fundamentals of music: six meters found most frequently in music; the rhythms common to these meters; tempo; dynamics; the major and minor mode; keys and their signatures; diatonic and chromatic tones; the basic elements of form; the principal and secondary chords; and the various symbols used in the notation of music. These have been introduced as needed for further growth, and they have been illustrated and applied in the melodies for singing and dictation.

The present chapter is somewhat of a summary of what has gone before, but in a new setting—a sort of coda, with a different treatment of material. For example, heretofore we have experienced rhythm only in a simple fashion as it occurs in the melody line; in this chapter we will consider it in a more complex form, as it appears in connection with two or more parts. For example, one part may have two or more notes moving against a single note in another part.

Also, chords which we have studied were related to the tonic. We are now ready to consider chords which belong to different keys and how, by their use, we may change the key of a composition, or *modulate*, as it is called. It is by some such means that the church organist modulates smoothly from the key of one composition to that of another, and it is by such means that the key may be changed during the course of a composition. The possible modulations in music are almost endless, and the few introductory examples presented here are to the related keys:

Ex. 15-1

| Key of Tonic | Key of Subdominant | Key of Dominant | Relative Minor of Tonic | Relative Minor of Subdominant | Relative Minor of Dominant |

We are already familiar with the terms used in Ex. 15-1 from our study of attendant scales and keys, and recall that scales and keys are said to be related in proportion to the number of tones common between them. For example, F♯ is the only different tone between the scales of C and G (and G's relative minor, E), and the only different tone between C and F (and F's relative minor, D) is B♭. It will also be observed that the degrees shown in Ex. 15-1 as *key tones* are the same as those upon which we have built the tonic, subdominant, dominant, submediant, supertonic, and mediant. As *key tones,* we may now identify them by the terms above.

For the beginner, a formula for modulating from the tonic to its related keys may prove helpful:

Key of the tonic	Modulating chord in new key resolved to tonic (new)	Cadence in the new key to establish firmly the change
A chord common to both the old and new keys	V₇ I[1]	IV I⁶₄ V₇ I

Observe the application of this formula in the examples which follow.

Ex. 15-2

[1] Chords other than this may be used. These introductory examples employ only the familiar dominant seventh. The modulations are approached from only one position of the tonic chord, and no inversions are used except the tonic six-four in the cadence.

To Relative Minor of Dominant
C to E Minor

I V₇ I IV I⁶₄ V₇ I
   Em

In the study of these modulations it is necessary to keep in mind that beginning with the second chord, the dominant seventh, all Roman numerals refer to the new key. Applying the formula to (a) (b) (c) (d) (e) (f) (g) above:

(a) Common chord: tonic in C, dominant in F.
(b) Modulating chord: dominant seventh in the new key, F.
(c) Tonic chord in new key.
(d-g) Cadence in the new key.

In like manner, apply the formula to the remaining modulations above, as well as to those which follow with F as the key of the tonic.

Ex. 15-3

| Key of Tonic | Key of Subdominant | Key of Dominant | Relative Minor of Tonic | Relative Minor of Subdominant | Relative Minor of Dominant |

Ex. 15-4

To Key of Subdominant
F to B Flat

To Key of Dominant
F to C

I V₇ I IV I⁶₄ V₇ I
   B Flat

I V₇ I IV I⁶₄ V₇ I
   C

To Relative Minor of Tonic
F to D Minor

To Relative Minor of Subdominant
F to G Minor

I V₇ I IV I⁶₄ V₇ I
   Dm

I V₇ I IV I⁶₄ V₇ I
   Gm

To Relative Minor of Dominant
F to A Minor

I   V₇   I   IV   I⁶₄   V₇   I
Am

Can you identify the modulations below?

Ex. 15-5

Identify the temporary modulations in the following melody:

Ex. 15-6

214

How Can I Leave Thee   Kucken

Singing in two parts. The new settings, or new experiences of what the student has already learned in past chapters, constitute part singing. The first ten melodies that the student will consider are in two parts. In his singing of these melodies he should listen carefully for several effects:

(1) For the intervals as the parts are sung, observing the total effect produced.

(2) For the rhythmic activity of each part as two or more notes in one part are sung against one note in the other.

(3) For repetitions as each part takes his turn in stating, at a higher or lower pitch, what the other has just finished singing. Repetitions are particularly noticeable in melodies 9 and 10. These correspond to exact or sequential repetitions found in melody, but their use here is known as *imitation.* That is, the voices or parts imitate each other.

Four part melodies. Four part singing likewise presents a new experience featuring familiar material.

(1) In former chapters the chords were played as the melodies were sung. Now we will hear them as the parts are sung, observing the total effect.

(2) The student should look for the passing and neighboring tones and observe their movement up and down as they move in similar directions. It should also be noted that they move in contrary directions—that is, one part moves up as the other moves down. These are known respectively as *parallel* and *contrary* motions.

(3) In his listening in four part singing, the student should be particularly concerned with the total effect produced by the major and minor chords. He should strive to become conscious of the other parts also being sung.

(4) At the end of each of the first two phrases of melody No. 12, the chord seems hollow or incomplete. The student should try to discover the

missing chord tone. If the last chord of this melody comes as a surprise, the student should try to determine why.

(5) The student will note the use of the VII triad in melodies 13 and 14. This chord appears with less frequency than the other triads introduced in this text. It is a diminished chord, its third being minor and its fifth diminished.

Melodies for Singing

3 Moderato

Lutheran Hymn

4 Andante

Chanson du Roi de Navarre (Unknown)

5   Moderato

Luther's Prayer (Lutheran)

6   Andante

Chanson MACHAUT

To The Blessed Trinity (Unknown)

Sweet Nymph Come to Thy Lover   MORLEY

9   Andantino

I Go Before My Darling   MORLEY

10 Slow

mp

I   V III VI   III IV I   VI III IV II   II6 V   I I

Essex's Last Good-Night   ENGLISH BALLAD

V   III II I IV   I6 I   IV V I I

11 Moderato

mf

I   I6 I V   I   I(F)

223

Daphne ENGLISH BALLAD

12 Moderato

Once I Loved a Maiden Fair   ENGLISH BALLAD

13   Moderato

Vive le Roy   ENGLISH BALLAD

14 Allegro

I   I₆ IV I   V I   I   I₆   II₆ V I

I   IV   I   V I   I   II   I   II₆ V I

Half Hannikin   English Dance

I   IV   I   V I   I   II   I   II₆ V I

15 Allegro

I   I₆   II   I   I₆ IV III₆ V I

226

Stand Thy Ground   Old Harry   English Dance

VI   VI   VI I6 II   I   I6 IV III6 V   I

Appendix

The Fundamentals of Conducting

In addition to the suggestions given in the body of the text regarding the movement of the hand or baton, the beginner should also master the following:

Fractional part of the beat. (1) When the music begins on a *fractional part of a beat,* give the preparatory beat, and, with a quick motion of the wrist, indicate when the ensemble is to begin. The breath, as usual, will be taken on the preparatory beat, but will be quicker. It must be remembered that the preparatory beat and any rhythmic cue indications must be in tempo.

The fermata. (2) The *fermata* or hold (⌢) should offer no particular problem. Merely bring the hand to a halt on the beat to be held; release in the direction of this beat, and the hand is in position for the beat which follows. Take as an example:

Praise God from Whom all bless ings flow

The fermata occurs on count three; stop the hand there. Just before the release, slightly raise the hand and release in the direction of the third beat. The hand is then in position for the fourth beat. The release actually marks the end of the third beat and rebounds as a beat should. It is this rebound which serves as a preparatory beat on which the ensemble breathes, thus preparing the group to sing or play on the fourth beat.

The left hand.   (3) The *left hand* should be used to indicate the entrance of various voices or instruments. Such indications should be preceded by the preparatory beat in the left hand so that the performer is made ready. In the case of successive entrances, it is wise to drop the left hand to the side after each entrance. This will make the left hand noticeable when another cue is to be executed.

Both hands.   (4) In leading community, assembly, or church congregational singing, or in directing large groups, the use of *both hands* may be employed. The hands should be spread apart suggesting an invitation for all the people to participate. The motion of the hands should be *down-up* for duple meter; *down-out-up* for triple; *down-in-out-up* for quadruple. The size of the beat will depend upon the size of the group and the tempo of the music.

The conductor.   The Conductor is an *interpreter* and a *leader.* This means that he must effectively explain—he must unfold or make clear the meaning of the music and know the techniques of developing through the music an ensemble expression. In doing this he must concern himself with three entities, the *composer,* the *ensemble,* and *himself.* His task is to *discover* and to *develop* to the utmost the beauty and feeling through himself and the performers as originally intended by the composer.

The composer.   The *composer* is the *first* consideration of the conductor. As interpreter the conductor should:

(1) Determine the *mood* of the music. This results from a combination of the *rhythm, melody, harmony, form, dynamics* and general tone color of the composition.

(2) Ascertain the *style* and *period* through which the composer has expressed himself. When did the composer live, how did he and other composers and artists of his period express themselves?

(3) Fathom the *real meaning* and *emotional levels* contained in the composition. What was the composer really endeavoring to say? His only means of communication was through a group of symbols which at best could only partly convey the real meaning. The conductor must "read between the lines," as it were, in order to ascertain the depth of meaning and feeling expressed in the composition. In this, the conductor's intelligence, imagination, and artistry are put to the test.

(4) *Study* and *analyze* each phrase and each voice part considering their relationship to other parts, determining, in other words, where the composer has best expressed himself, and where he has placed emphasis.

(5) Examine the *dynamics* to determine the relative loudness and softness of voice parts, phrases, and other divisions of the composition.

The ensemble. The *second* consideration for the conductor is the *ensemble* through which he conveys the composer's message. The problems confronting him are:

(1) Does the ensemble have the *background* and *musical ability* to interpret this composition effectively? Is the vocal or instrumental range suitable for this group? Can the ensemble properly execute the rhythm, melody, harmony, and tempo? Can the group fathom the deeper meaning of the music? Will the music challenge the ensemble sufficiently to sustain interest? Does the ensemble have the necessary voices and instruments to emphasize effectively the parts stressed by the composer?

(2) Brief *explanation* of his concept of the composition as a result of his study. When the ensemble is more familiar with the composition, the conductor will ask stimulating questions in an effort to lead each member to understand, feel, and interpret the music.

(3) Develop the *tone quality* or variety of qualities in keeping with the character of the music and/or text. Too often, notes are merely sung or played, regardless of whether the music is bright, gloomy, prayerful, or speaks of love, hope, or hate. Improvement in tone quality is often the result of a thorough understanding of music and text.

(4) Work out *phrasing, breathing,* changes in *tempos,* and *dynamics.*

(5) Concern himself with *balance of parts, pitch, intonation, blend,* correct use of *vowels* and *consonants, attacks,* and *releases.*

Thus, in meeting these requirements the conductor must understand thoroughly both the music and the ensemble, and must unfold to his listeners the hidden beauties of each: the composer's through a sympathetic interpretation of his music, that of the ensemble through a proper attention to its vital, living personality. In the latter respect, he must be skillful in human relationships. Attitude, response, understanding, and cooperation of the participators with him in the composer's music are of great importance.

Himself. Yet, although the personality of each individual is important, the stress in this brief discussion must be primarily on the conductor. He is the *third* consideration.

The following outline will serve to suggest three important qualifications of a successful conductor:

(1) *Musicianship.*
    a. Historical and theoretical background of music.
    b. Fundamental principles of vocal and/or instrumental production as applied in the ensemble.
    c. A keen sense of rhythm.
    d. Ability to hear melodic and harmonic intervals.

(2) *Personality.*
  a. A wholesome, cheerful, positive attitude toward life, people, and music.
  b. Ability to see mistakes, including his own, in a humorous light.
  c. Self confidence blended with humility.
  d. Patience, patience, patience!

(3) *General Abilities.*
  a. An understanding of the individual and mass mind.
  b. The ability to inspire others.
  c. A creative imagination.
  d. An ability to organize.

In one sentence: the conductor must be a *musician,* a *psychologist,* and an *organizer,* possessing all of those personal qualities which *pleasantly cause others to do his will.*

As may be easily seen, conducting involves far more than merely "beating time." Yet the conductor must also master—at least—the *conventional conducting patterns* for the various meters. These are the same for both choral and instrumental conducting. By the use of these patterns the conductor informs the ensemble where he is within the measure. Through the character of his beat, eyes, face, and his entire body, he reveals to the group the essential nature of the music. These expressions should be practiced before a mirror by the apprentice conductor until they become a definite part of his personality, wholly expressive of his feelings. Many a beginner endeavors to copy the idiosyncrasies of a conductor he admires. But if he is wise, he will find for himself as quickly as possible *his own personality* and thus *freedom* and *control* through these patterns. As with freedom under the law, freedom in this respect begins with control and discipline. He must therefore guard against developing habits which have no meaning, or which in any way attract undue attention to himself and consequently detract from the music.

While leading his group, the conductor should *stand erect* with the weight of the body on the soles of the feet. The over-all posture should be such as to convey *command, security,* and *confidence* to the conductor, performer, and audience. There should be no tension in the wrist, fingers, elbows, or shoulders. The arm should be held slightly away from the ribs and clearly visible to all performers. This position makes for more control and freedom of movement, expansion for breathing, and suggests animation.

Ten conducting precepts:
(1) The time value of tones is determined by the interval of time existing between the beats which extends from the beginning of the one count to the beginning of the next. In the following example, the release of the tied note should be on count two (the rest):

(2) The result of what happens between the beats is either good or bad music and may be indicative of the conductor's hand movements.

(3) The accompanyist should not play while the conductor is giving instructions and should begin only when signaled by him. At this point, the choir and conductor should give full attention, thus showing respect for the music and the accompanyist and gaining the attention of the audience. The attitude should indicate that the composition begins with the accompaniment and is not completed until the release of the final chord. The same attitude and attention should be accorded the soloist.

(4) When the conductor is wrong or makes a mistake, he should admit it. This is a mark of greatness which even small children sense.

(5) The appearance of a group is important from the standpoint of the audience as well as the group. A neat, clean appearance in attractive uniform dress may actually improve tone quality.

(6) Talk less; sing and play more.

(7) Make corrections in all sincerity; compliment and express appreciation to the ensemble.

(8) Sarcasm marks a conductor as "little" and comes back to him in a cynical group attitude and in a poor tone quality.

(9) The conductor should keep his eyes upon the group; and the ensemble should keep their eyes upon him.

(10) The conductor and the ensemble should thoroughly enjoy the activity if desirable vitality and an effect of spontaneity is created through the performance.

Index

233

R

Relationship of chords, 124, 125
Relationship of keys, 124, 125
Relationship of scales, 23, 39, 59, 124, 125
Relative minor scale, 91
Repeat dot, 171
Repeat signs (*See* Repeat dots, Da Capo, Dal Segno)
Repeated notes, 170
Repetition, 185
  exact, 59, 185
  sequence, 59
Rest, 7
Rest tone, 24
Rests, relative lengths, 7
Rhythm:
  definition, 14
  divided beat, 29, 30 (*See also* Melodies for Singing, Chapter 3)
  dotted-eighth-sixteenth, 113 (*See also* Melodies for Singing, Chapter 8)
  dotted-eighth-sixteenth in $\frac{6}{8}$ time, 130 (*See also* Melodies for Singing, Chapter 9)
  syncopation, 189, 190 (*See also* Melodies for Singing, Chapter 13)
  triplet, 144 (*See also* Melodies for Singing, Chapter 10)
Root (*See* Tonic, Dominant, etc.)

S

Scale, 6
  attendant, 59, 125
  chromatic, 198, 199
  formula, 20, 21, 22
  major, 20, 39
  major diatonic, 21
  melodic minor, 92, 93
  minor, 90, 91, 92, 107, 108
  modal, natural, pure minor, 92
  parallel major, 108
  parallel minor, 108
  relation of scale tones, 6
  relationship, 23, 39, 59, 124, 125
  relationship of scales, 23
  relative minor, 91
  resolution of active tones, 24
  syllable names, 8
  tone characteristics, 24
  tonic minor, 107, 108, 109
Scales:
  major, 58, 59
  relationship, 23, 39, 59, 124, 125
Secondary chords, 172
Semitone, 20 (*See also* Half Step)
Sequence, 59, 185
Sharp, 22, 198
  double, 198

Singing in parts, 215 (*See also* Melodies for Singing, Chapter 15)
Slur, 65, 167
Staccato, 168
Staff, 2, 3
  degrees, 3
  great, 4
  ledger lines, 3
  letter names, 3, 4
Subdivided beat, 96, 97 (*See also* Melodies for Singing, Chapter 7)
Subdominant chord:
  major, 61
  major key, 61, 62, 63
    inversions, 61
    neighboring tone, 62
    passing tone, 62
    positions, 61
    progressions, 62, 63, 64, 77, 78
  minor key, 127, 128 (*See also* Melodies for Singing, Chapter 9)
    inversions, 128
    neighboring tones, 128
    passing tones, 128
    positions, 128
    progressions, 128, 129
Submediant chord, 187 (*See also* Melodies for Singing, Chapter 13)
  inversions, 187
  positions, 187
Supertonic chord, 172 (*See also* Melodies for Singing, Chapter 12)
  inversions, 172, 173
  positions, 172, 173
Syncopation, 189, 190

T

Tempo, 73
  definition, 14
  terms, 74, 75
Tetrachord, 21
Tie, 45, 46, 65
Timbre, 1
Time, medium of expression, 1
Time signature, 10, 11
Tone:
  active, 24, 76
  characteristics, 1
  chromatic, 198, 199
  diatonic, 198, 199
  enharmonic, 60
  fundamental, 126, 127
  length, 1
  medium of expression, 1
  pitch, 1
  quantity, 1
  rest, 24
Tonic chord, 24, 25, 26